HARDPRESS.NET
HOME OF HARD-TO-FIND BOOKS

An Address to the Proprietors & Debenture Holders of the West Hartlepool Harbour and Railway Company by B. Coleman.

by Benjamin Coleman (Of Threadneedle St, London.)

Address:
HardPress
8345 NW 66TH ST #2561
MIAMI FL 33166-2626
USA
Email: info@hardpress.net

[*Second Edition.*]

AN ADDRESS

TO THE

PROPRIETORS & DEBENTURE HOLDERS

OF THE

WEST HARTLEPOOL

Harbour and Railway Company,

WITH

CORRESPONDENCE

AND

Report of a Meeting held at the London Tavern, on the 1st March, 1860.

PRINTED FOR AND PUBLISHED BY

B. COLEMAN, 28, THREADNEEDLE STREET,

LONDON.

Price One Shilling.

PRINTED BY THOMAS SCOTT, WARWICK COURT, HOLBORN.

TO THE

PROPRIETORS AND DEBENTURE HOLDERS

OF THE

West Hartlepool Harbour and Railway Company.

On the 12th and 24th of January, 1859, I had the honor of addressing letters to you avowedly for the purpose of calling your attention "To THE NECESSITY "OF ENQUIRING INTO THE PAST ADMINISTRATION AND "PRESENT FINANCIAL POSITION OF THE WEST HARTLEPOOL "HARBOUR AND RAILWAY COMPANY." I believe I had good grounds for sounding the alarm, though I was met with denial, misrepresentation, and abuse; but at length, with a show of openness and candour, but only *a show*, the directors of your Company were forced to yield the point for which I contended, namely, a COMMITTEE OF INVESTIGATION; and at the general meeting of 1859, they proposed, and the meeting appointed a Committee, called of "Assistance," but admittedly for the purpose, among other things, of testing whether the Company was, as represented by your directors, in a perfectly sound and prosperous condition, and whether your affairs had been judiciously and honestly administered. This committee, selected by your chairman, Mr. Ralph Ward Jackson, consisted of five gentlemen who were the least likely to trouble themselves, and who, with one exception, least able to investigate the accounts of a large and intricately-constituted public Company. One of them, Mr. Birley, had *privately* intimated to Mr. Jackson, before he left the meeting, that he would not act. Another, Mr. Nicholas Wood, has, under special arrangements, large transactions with your company. The third, Admiral Cator, is the personal friend of Mr. Jackson, and not a man of business. The fourth, Mr. Baynes, is an auditor of the company, who, if there were errors in the accounts, would not be less responsible to you than than the directors themselves; and the fifth member of this committee, Mr. Thomas Sturge, is a gentleman of known wealth and great commercial experience; but who, from his advanced years, and living 300 miles away from West Hartlepool, was, perhaps, the least likely of any of the five nominees of the chairman to trouble himself with the labour of investigating accounts, but whose advice, when asked, would no doubt be most valuable, and who could accept the appointment which he might otherwise have declined, because of the designation of this committee, which, as I have said, was called a "Committee of Assistance" or "Consultation," for the purpose, as stated in the directors' report of 1859, of assisting the directors "with their advice as to the best mode of disposing of the surplus property of the Company, and to co-operate with them generally on the interests of the Company."

It was also stated in this report, that in consequence of "certain attacks having been publicly made upon "your chairman and directors," they had invited "some influential proprietors (who are present at this "meeting) to attend at West Hartlepool, and examine "into them (the accounts?). Such proprietors have "done so, and your directors need scarcely say that "the result has been that those proprietors have "expressed their entire satisfaction with the honour "and uprightness of the administration of its affairs "by the chairman and directors."

This statement, however, was not borne out by the proceedings. I put this question—

"You state that you have submitted the accounts "to some influential proprietors. May I ask you their "names?—

"Chairman. Mr. Sturge, Dr. De Vitre, Mr. Hudson "of Kendal, and others."

Mr. Sturge was silent. Dr. De Vitre said that "he "had not been invited to examine into the accounts. "He was not an accountant."

Mr. Hudson did not say anything at that moment, but at a subsequent period of the meeting, when seconding a prepared resolution proposed by Admiral Cator (who by the way had advised the chairman not to answer any of my questions as to figures, "the less "said about figures the better for them all," was his innocent but significant remark), Mr. Hudson did say, he "being an accountant by profession, could speak "positively as to the accuracy of the accounts by the "books, and of course he did not enquire further." He also said he had "been in West Hartlepool since "Wednesday morning," just 48 hours.

The meeting passed various resolutions, which had been previously prepared, of a highly complimentary character, which were duly advertised by the directors; and the press, in the interest of Mr. Jackson, devoted columns in terms of high eulogium on his spotless character, and congratulation on his having passed through a trying ordeal scatheless from the attacks of a vindictive libeller, who had propagated a series of malicious and unfounded falsehoods.

They did not know, nor did Mr. Jackson, that before the meeting separated Mr. Sturge, who had at the commencement of the proceedings taken a decided part against me, had come to my side to whisper in my ear that he should like to have some talk with me on the subject of my charges, and that I had in consequence arranged to meet him for that purpose on my return to London. I was thus prevented from proceeding at once to vindicate myself from the odium which Mr. Jackson, through the press and privately, was most industriously heaping upon me, and you will see from a perusal of the correspondence which follows this statement, the reason why I have been unable to do so until this moment.

Within a week after the meeting I wrote to Mr. Sturge to say I should be glad to see him. He came accordingly to my office and spent just five hours at our first interview, and three hours at our second, which took place two or three days afterwards.

The nature of our conversation I will endeavour to give you briefly, and I again refer you to the correspondence for a corroboration of my statements. It was substantially to this effect—Mr. Sturge said, "I am a proprietor of about £30,000 of the Clarence "preference stock, and my family and myself hold together about £50,000. I know all about West "Hartlepool. I negotiated the sale of the Clarence "Railway with Jackson years ago, when Pease of Darlington was about to buy it, and Jackson stepped in. "I know all all about the Collieries, and I think I have "as much influence over Jackson as any man. I have "had in my time quite enough to do with commercial "questions. I am now advanced in years; have no need "to trouble myself, and never intended to take upon "myself any labour again; but with your charges "against this concern, I have made up my mind, if you "will show me a sufficient case, to probe it to the "bottom, even at the risk of losing all I have invested in "it," &c. Mr. Sturge also gave a very honourable reason for his desire to know the truth. He said, "I would "not think of selling any part of my stock to throw the "burden on others whilst I had any doubt of its value."

On Mr. Sturge's second visit to my office he told me he had telegraphed for Mr. Jackson, and had seen him, and had told him of his intention to go into this investigation, at which Mr. Jackson had expressed his perfect satisfaction and willingness to facilitate it.

I gave to Mr. Sturge a book (which has been recently returned, at my request, by Mr. Bell,* who said, "*it had not been of any use to Mr. Sturge*," in which I had written up the leading facts I had collected in proof of my allegations.

---

* Mr. Alfred Bell, it must be understood, has acted in a threefold capacity. He is Mr. Sturge's private solicitor, he is Mr. Jackson's private solicitor, and he is the solicitor to the West Hartlepool Company, and Mr. Jackson uses Mr. Bell's offices as his town address.

MR. STURGE THEN SAID, "NOW YOU MUST NOT SAY
" NOR WRITE ANOTHER WORD AT PRESENT; wait until I
" have made myself master of the case. It will take
" some time; you must not be too anxious; I have a
" first-rate man whom I shall send down to inspect the
" property, and as my sister is in delicate health, I
" shall probably take her when the fine weather comes
" and stay with her at Seaton, (a small watering place
" near West Hartlepool,) and look after matters on the
" spot," &c., &c.

I expressed myself quite satisfied with this arrangement. I said I would make any temporary sacrifice, in the confidence that if he went into the enquiry with his known ability for the task, he *must* corroborate all I had ever said. It will be seen that in the early stage of his investigation, I had but little correspondence with Mr. Sturge, but after a month or two, I met him occasionally at the office of Messrs. Eykyn Brothers, and at one of these interviews he made a remarkable admission, which was the first intimation I had of the seriousness of his discoveries. I was pressing him to tell me how he was getting on, and he said, "very well; I have got the books and papers at my house, but I am obliged to proceed very cautiously. *It is necessary that I should take the measure of this man's mind, and do nothing hastily or abruptly, lest he should do something that would defeat my object.* You must rest satisfied with the assurance that you will be exonerated from making false charges." I was also told by Mr. Gardner, the accountant, who had been at Mr. Sturge's house, that Mr. Sturge had told him I had nothing to apprehend from the result of his enquiries.

TO THIS EXPLANATION, I BEG TO ADD THAT FROM THE MOMENT OF HIS TAKING THE CASE IN HAND, NEITHER MR. STURGE, MR. BELL, NOR ANY ONE OF THE COMMITTEE UP TO THE PRESENT MOMENT, HAS EVER EXPRESSED A DOUBT OF THE TRUTHFULNESS OF MY CHARGES, NOR HAVE THEY EVER ASKED ME TO PROVE ANY ONE OF THEM.

It is most important that you should bear this fact in mind, as it not only speaks volumes in itself, but it goes directly to disprove the unjust expressions of Mr. G. W. Rowley, made by him at the last meeting, and received with cheers, that "Mr. Coleman had had a "whole year to substantiate his charges and had failed "in everything." Whatever may be said to the contrary, there is no doubt that the investigation of the Company's affairs was, from first to last, carried on by Mr. Sturge alone, with the assistance of Mr. Alfred Bell, and that not one of the other members of the committee, took as might have been expected, any step to discharge their duty, nor knew anything of the report until it was completed.

The result as you know, was, that a report dated December 20, 1859,—two months before the meeting—was handed to Mr. Jackson, which "thanks Mr. "Coleman for calling their particular attention to the "position of the Company," *but which is entirely silent as to the nature of my charges*, and this report is only made public on the day of the meeting when the proprietors were asked to give their sanction to a Bill now before Parliament, which seeks to raise the capital of the Company by an increase of several hundred thousand pounds, without any explanation being offered. Mr. Jackson, the chairman, in the absence of Mr. Sturge and Mr. Bell, not being able, as he said, to explain such portions of the Report and Bill as were questioned.*

As the whole of this part of the subject was clearly put by Mr. Wilkinson at the meeting of share and bond holders, held recently at the London Tavern, and now printed in the appendix, I need do no more than refer you to it, assuring you that it deserves your earnest and attentive perusal.

Mr. Jackson, in his printed letter, addressed to you on the 18th of January, 1859, opens up the circum-

* I asked whether the £3,400,000 was *all* the Bill proposed. Whether it was not with borrowing powers £4,500,000. Mr. Jackson said "*he did not so understand it.*" Another proprietor said he thought I was right. Mr. Jackson then said the copies we had of the Bill were not the same as his. The Bill had been altered, and that made the difference in our views, (see report of general meeting). *I have ascertained since my return to London that Mr. Jackson's statement is not true, there has been no alteration in the Bill.*

stances of his brother Edwin's connexion and disputes with me, and he thus relieves me from the voluntary restraint I had imposed on myself of not speaking again of that unhappy case, which, as he says, "was "entirely unconnected with the West Hartlepool "undertaking," and therefore I think ought not to have been obtruded by him upon your notice. But as he has done so for the purpose of establishing a claim on your sympathies with a high-minded act of disinterested generosity, to which he is not entitled, and of lowering me in your estimation, I am compelled to advert to it, though I shall do so very briefly, referring those of you who are not already acquainted with the history, to a pamphlet published by me in 1858, which fully describes the conduct of Mr. Edwin Ward Jackson, whom I charged with writing a number of anonymous letters, addressed to several of my friends, containing the grossest imputations on my commercial and moral character, and who, although he was assisted in his defence by the most super-human efforts and most improper conduct of Mr. Ralph Ward Jackson, was nevertheless found guilty, and sentenced to pay to me £400 damages and £480 costs.

In Mr. Jackson's letter to you, he says of me that, "By publishing and circulating among our relations, "friends and neighbours, printed pamphlets reflecting "most harshly upon my brother Edwin for not paying "the alleged debt of honour, Mr. Coleman so dis-"turbed the peace of mind of my aged mother, my "brother's wife, and other members of the family, "that we felt if we could reasonably satisfy ourselves "that that debt could be adjusted, and the sore and "annoyance to the family be annihilated, we would "recommend my brother to settle the matter with Mr. "Coleman, in order to a permanent peace," &c.

In a letter addressed to a friend of mine by Mr. Ralph Jackson, through whom he was endeavouring to conciliate me, dated October 26, 1858, he says—

"I have consulted with other members of my "family on the subject, not one of whom, including

"myself, have any knowledge whatever of the parti-
"culars of the transactions between Mr. Coleman and
"our brother Edwin, on which this remaining debt
"of honour is based," &c.

This letter was written four months after I had published *the only pamphlet I had ever written on this or any other subject*, not one of which had I ever sent to any member of Mr. Jackson's family, nor to any one known to them, nor in fact to any one residing in the county of Durham. It was circulated only and sold through the booksellers as any other book would be; and if this be so, I hope it entirely satisfies you that I was not guilty of the meanness of "disturbing the "peace of mind of his aged mother, *by circulating* "*printed pamphlets*," *&c.*, which Mr. Jackson, in order to divert your attention from the real points in issue, so unjustly charges me with doing.

At the last meeting of the West Hartlepool Company, I asked Mr. Jackson whether he meant now to say that the collieries and steam boats belonged to the West Hartlepool Company, and he replied, "cer-"tainly, and they have done so for several years."

You are no doubt aware that one of the original charges I made against the chairman was, that your monies were being used for the support of collieries and steam boats which belonged to him and others.*

In a letter he addressed to me in reply, on the 20th December, 1858, he says, "I have to state to you "that the West Hartlepool Company do not possess, "directly or indirectly, one inch of coal property in "the kingdom, and that they have no responsibility "or connection whatever with the working of any "such property; neither have I or any other director "ever derived from or asked the Company to benefit "any one of us by any means of that sort, either as "respects collieries, steamers, or any other description "of property whatever."

These are two notable specimens of Mr. Jackson's

* These collieries and steamboats were registered in various names, and divided into parts or shares, of which Mr. R. W. Jackson held the largest number.

disingenuousness; and as I am still assailed by Mr. Jackson through the press in such terms as these—taken from the *Durham County Advertiser*, of the 2nd instant,—"There are people in this world whom no "exposure, no disgrace, no expressions of public con-"tempt, however clearly deserved, can put down," &c. &c. And as Mr. Jackson is still labouring to fix a stain on *my* character, I may as well give you the advantage which I possess of appreciating *his*, by which you will be enabled to judge whether he is deserving of the high encomiums which are passed at his meetings, and paraded in public advertisements at your expense; and whether he is the man to be entrusted with the unlimited control of three or four millions of your money.*

Some time ago, before a Parliamentary Committee which was sitting on the West Durham line, Mr. Jackson was asked if he had ever acted as Secretary to the West Hartlepool Company? He answered, "Never."

Have bonds ever been issued which were not included in your accounts? Answer, "Never."

These questions were repeated, and still answered in the negative.

The Counsel then produced bonds of the West Hartlepool Company for £60,000, bearing Mr. Ralph Jackson's signature as secretary, and which had been given for the purchase of collieries, and were not included in the Company's accounts.

It is not recorded that Mr. Alfred Bell, who stood by Mr. Jackson's side, fainted at this exposure, or that Mr. Jackson himself sunk abashed to the floor, but it is stated that, turning on the solicitor who was conducting the case, Mr. Jackson coolly charged him "with a gross breach of professional confidence."

Some years ago, Mr. Jackson had large money transactions with Mr. Thomas Friend Dickinson, of Newcastle-on-Tyne, who was afterwards appointed manager for the Whitworth Colliery, which was purchased by Captain Vernon. Dickinson died suddenly,

* The Directors are Mr. Jackson, his father-in-law, his son, Mr. Watson, and Mr. Wigham, who is very infirm *and blind.*—*See* Appendix, p. 45.

and a claim was then made by Mr. Jackson on Captain Vernon for about £28,000. This was disputed. A bill was filed against Mr. Jackson by Captain Vernon, and it resulted in Mr. Jackson paying a large sum, either in money or an annuity secured to Captain Vernon.

John Robson, a viewer of collieries, was put forward by Mr. Ralph Jackson to purchase collieries, and was jointly engaged with him and George Hunter, both men of humble origin in large colliery transactions. Hunter died, as did Robson some time after. Their widows thought they were left well provided for; but Mr. Jackson brought a claim against the collieries for an enormous sum, it is said £180,000, which swamped them. This too was disputed. Mr. Tiplady, solicitor, of Durham, acting, as I have been told, for the widows, it resulted in a compromise by Mr. Jackson securing to each an annuity.

Mr. T. C. Gibson had large transactions with Mr. Ralph Jackson, in collieries and steam boats, and he has a large pension secured in some shape by Mr. Jackson.

The transaction alluded to by me at the last meeting, and which you will see by the published report, I dared Mr. Jackson, Mr. Sturge, or Mr. Bell, to put me to the proof of, was this:—Messrs. ——— of London, had several £1,000 bonds, five per cent. of the West Hartlepool Company sent to them, as collateral security, by the manager of Mr. Jackson's collieries.

Some time after it occurred to them to ask the value of the bonds, and as there was no price in the London market, they requested a friend at Newcastle to make enquiries as to the value of five per cent. West Hartlepool bonds. The reply was, "I have spoken to "Mr. Drewry, the share broker, and he says *he* "*cannot tell without seeing them.*" Messrs. ——— therefore sent one of the bonds to their friend, and he wrote to say Mr. Drewry *had asked him to leave it with him for a day.* My informants presumed that Mr. Drewry had shown this bond to Mr. Jackson, as they received in course of post, a letter enclosing a cheque from Mr. Jackson for the whole amount, and complaining that they should have offered these bonds for sale, which, however, they had not done.

These bonds, I am informed, had not any numbers, and you will now understand the object of a question I asked on this head, at the general meeting of 1859.

As Mr. Drewry very emphatically denied any knowledge of this transaction at the last meeting, I am bound to believe that Messrs. ——— must have been misinformed as to the name of the broker. But of the transaction itself there is no mistake. *I saw Mr. Jackson's letter which enclosed the cheque.*

There are other transactions in which Mr. Jackson has been engaged, which, in considering the moral worth of the man, who asks for your continued confidence, would weigh heavily against him, but as they do not belong to the affairs of your Company I refrain from recording them.

The whole of the foregoing statements were contained in the book I gave to Mr. Sturge, which he handed to Mr. Alfred Bell; and yet, as I have said, neither of them has asked me a single question on the subject, whilst Mr. Bell encourages such men as Mr. Rowley,* whom he sent primed to the meeting at the London Tavern, to proclaim to the world that "all "my charges against Mr. Jackson failed after having "had 12 months to substantiate them."

You will see by the correspondence how anxiously I have endeavoured to avoid the necessity of being again prominent in this West Hartlepool controversy. You will also see how impossible it is for me to be silent under the disappointment occasioned by Mr. Sturge's report, when my character for common honesty and good feeling is at stake. Mr. Jackson and his adherents still endeavour to persuade you that this is a question entirely of personal animosity against him on my part, and Mr. Rowley was especially soli-

---

* Mr. Rowley was angry with me at this meeting for doubting his denial of partizanship, and afterwards proved it by first trying to correct Mr. Wilkinson as to the amount of bonds held by Mr. W., and then of producing the private letters which had passed between him and Mr. Bell.

citous to enforce this view at the late meeting. But surely it is needless for me to state that this is to raise a false issue altogether. My feelings towards Mr. Jackson are not matters for your consideration, nor have I ever obtruded them upon your attention,—although repeatedly provoked to do so. The *facts* I have alleged, and am prepared to maintain against the management of the Company, and the peril in which it is thereby placed—are, I respectfully submit, the only questions for the Shareholders. Not that I shrink from any investigation of the personal matter. On the contrary, I have more than once publicly declared I am quite ready to enter into that if necessary, and at the same time to lay before you a remarkable correspondence of recent date (not yet made public), between a friend of mine, Mr. Jackson, and myself, in which Mr. Jackson expresses a high regard for my character. And all that I deem it permissible now to state on that point is, THAT IN THE WHOLE COURSE OF A 30 YEARS' EXPERIENCE IN THE COMMERCIAL WORLD, I HAVE NEVER BEEN INVOLVED IN A SERIOUS QUARREL WITH ANY MAN, AND THAT I HAVE NEVER SUED, COERCED, NOR TAKEN LEGAL PROCEEDINGS AGAINST ANY MAN EXCEPT MR. JACKSON'S BROTHER EDWIN, whom Mr. Jackson aided and abetted to the utmost of his power, despite my earnest efforts to satisfy him of his error,—and whom, when I had signally defeated and disgraced, Mr. Jackson openly repudiated.

I am, your obedient Servant,

BENJAMIN COLEMAN.

28, Threadneedle Street,
London, March, 1860.

Some time past, before a Parliamentary committee sitting on the Durham and Cleveland Railway Bill, the West Hartlepool Company sought for powers to subscribe £60,000.

MR. GEO. BIDDER, C. E., was examined, and asked "if he had examined the West Hartlepool Company's financial position?"

Answer—"Yes, and I have come to a very strong conclusion on that point. It just depends on how long they can stave off an investigation into their accounts. Indeed, I am quite certain 'that there is something rotten in the state of Denmark.' If their position was sound their accounts would be furnished in a very different shape."

CORRESPONDENCE.

March 5th, 1859.

Dear Sir,—The *Railway Times*, *Mining Journal*, and *Durham Advertiser*, of this day, contain leading articles reflecting very hard upon me, with the usual amount of one-sided disingennousness. But acting on your advice, I do not intend to make a reply to any of these partizan-dictated censures.

I enclose a leading article, taken from the *Durham Chronicle*, of an opposite character, to which I invite your attention; containing, as it does, some complimentary remarks on yourself.

I am leaving home to-day,—my address for the next week will be at Dr. Wilson's Malvern, Worcestershire.

I have reason, under the express assurances you have given me, to be quite satisfied with the present position, and of the ultimate result of the West Hartlepool controversy.

Your position is much like what mine was, with the difference of the influencing cause. I pledged my honour that I would investigate the affairs of that Company, on being shewn good grounds for so doing. Ralph Jackson came forward *after* I had so bound myself, to redeem the wrong his brother had done me, though he had withstood all my urgent appeals to him to intercede for many months *previously*.

It is thought by some, that as Ralph *did* at length do what was right to me, I ought not to have proceeded with my invidious task. But I felt, whilst I had such undeniable facts to go upon, I could no more have withdrawn in honour, though tempted by a sum of money most acceptable to me, than you could withdraw by the offer of a bribe; which was the only light in which I could view Jackson's disposition to pay this old debt of his brother Edwin's, after all that has passed between us.

You will see by my letter of the 10th November, 1858, in the correspondence you have, that I distinctly refused to receive the £710 with any condition that I should be silent on the West Hartlepool affairs. But Jackson has, in his letter to the shareholders, tried to make it appear that *I did* a dishonourable act by receiving the money, and then attacking him afterwards.

My anxiety not to labour under the disadvantage of any mistake on this point in your mind, will, I hope, plead my excuse in troubling you with this explanation.

I am, dear Sir, yours respectfully,
(Signed) Benj. Coleman.

Mr. Thomas Sturge.

Northfleet, March 10, 1859.

Dear Sir,—Having had a conversation with Mr. Sturge, and he having read me part of your letter to him of the 15th instant, you may be glad to know he much regrets the insertion of these articles you allude to. He thinks, when left unanswered, they cease the sooner, and he sincerely hopes that these may be the last unpleasant remarks that may be made, and that you will not allow your mind to be disturbed by them.

I am, yours truly,
(Signed) Geo. Enderby.

B. Coleman, Esq.

Northfleet, July 1st, 1859.

Dear Sir,—Mr. Sturge proposed to be in town tomorrow, and will be at Eykyn Brothers, Change Alley,

Cornhill, at a quarter before eleven o'clock, and will be able to give you half an hour's conversation.

Yours truly, dear Sir,
(Signed) GEO. ENDERBY.

B. Coleman, Esq.

London, July 5, 1859.

My dear Sir,—With reference to our conversation of Saturday last, on the subject of West Hartlepool affairs, I desire to place on record the feeling I verbally expressed on the fact you then communicated to me, that your researches were being prosecuted with the co-operation of Mr. Bell, of the firm of Bell, Steward & Lloyd.

The charges I have made against Mr. Ralph Ward Jackson, and the general management of West Hartlepool Dock and Railway Company, are very grave. They are, I take it, to be confirmed or disproved by the result of your present enquiries.

Messrs. Bell, Steward & Lloyd have been for many years the professional advisers of Mr. Jackson. Mr. Bell stood by the side of Mr. Jackson at the late general meeting of the West Dock Company, actively prompting him, and was the only man present, as far as I could judge from his looks and manner, who hurled defiance at my statements, and gave thereby a tone to the already heavily-charged prejudice against me. These statements, I am certain you will now find, are *substantially true*, whilst I am equally confident all Mr. Jackson's affirmations and denials made at that meeting, which by his manner Mr. Bell endorsed, you will find, are substantially *false!*

Messrs. Bell, Steward & Lloyd have no doubt been professionally engaged in the several suits brought against Mr. Jackson, which have been settled without coming before the public. They were, I know, in the Chancery suit promoted against Mr. Jackson by the Trustees of Christ Church, West Hartlepool, which caused so much scandal in that town; and in a word, I assume the firm as his professional advisers, are thoroughly cognisant of all the worst features of Mr. Jackson's parliamentary tactics and financial policy.

I therefore naturally felt surprised when I heard that these same gentlemen had, as it were, *my* case in hand against *their* client, not seeing how it is possible they can do justice to both parties.*

In obedience to your wishes, and in the confidence that the matter of probing the West Dock Company's affairs could not be in better hands, I have remained silent since the general meeting of February last, bearing meantime, the odium of having made false and unfounded charges against Mr. Jackson and his management, from which I look to be relieved and entirely exonerated by your report to the shareholders.

It is my intention to wait any reasonable time for your statement. The facilities which you say have been given to you by all connected with the Company, which have already made you better acquainted with the real state of the Company's affairs than any one else, induces me to hope I may learn something of your views very shortly.

There may be advantages in employing gentlemen standing so high in the profession as Messrs. Bell & Co., who have so intimate a knowledge of West Hartlepool affairs, which I cannot see and appreciate; and all I now wish to convey to you without presuming to question your discretion is, that if from any cause your report should not embrace a confirmation of my allegations, I shall hold myself at liberty to pursue any course which the vindication of my character may require hereafter.†

Assuring you in the meantime of my entire con-

---

* Mr. Jackson stated at the last general meeting, that he had seen my correspondence with Mr. Sturge,—my fears, it will be seen, were therefore not unfounded.

† Mr. Sturge answered my objections in a personal interview. He said I was mistaken, Mr. Bell knew more than any other man of West Hartlepool affairs, and had great influence over Mr. Jackson. Mr. Bell had been his family's adviser for many years, and he had great faith in his integrity. "You may depend upon his doing what is strictly just," &c.

fidence in the integrity of your motives, and of your special ability for the task you have undertaken,

I am, my dear Sir, yours faithfully,

(Signed) BENJ. COLEMAN.

Mr. Thos. Sturge.

28, Threadneedle Street, July 14th, 1859.

My dear Sir,—I had the pleasure of addressing you on the 5th instant, which I hope you duly received; since then I have seen two gentlemen, from whom I have obtained some important information corroborative of some points embraced in my charges against Mr. Jackson's policy, which, if you desire to hear, I shall be glad to give you.*

Some time since, Mr. Basnett, the secretary of the West Dock Company, promised to let me know the decision of his board, as to my application for a list of the shareholders, but he has not done so. I should like to have this list, but forbear to press for it without your sanction. You may perhaps have it, and not object to my seeing it, and taking a copy for myself.†

When it is convenient, and you desire to meet me, be so good as to inform me, addressed to my private residence, which will enable me to attend to your appointment.

Dear Sir, yours faithfully,

(Signed) BENJ. COLEMAN.

Mr. Thos. Sturge, Northfleet.

Northfleet House, July 20th, 1859.

Sir,—Mr. Sturge wishes me to say that he regrets that your notes should with others, have remained so long unanswered, owing to his engagements. It is

---

* In an interview I had shortly after the date of this letter, I reminded Mr. Sturge of the "important information," but he said he did not care to know it."

† I have applied several times for this list, once since the last meeting, but I cannot obtain it.

necessary for him to proceed carefully, cautiously and patiently, in the work he has undertaken,—and he makes no doubt the shareholders of the Company generally will be satisfied with his conduct, and in that number he includes yourself.

He thinks it unadvisable for you just now to press for a list of shareholders; should circumstances hereafter arise to make it necessary, there is no doubt you will obtain it without much difficulty.

I am, sir, yours respectfully,
(Signed) SARAH SELINA BOYES.

To Mr. B. Coleman.

July 23, 1859.

My dear Sir,—I am obliged by the receipt of your note of the 21st instant, and as you think it undesirable, I shall not press for a list of the West Hartlepool Proprietors.

Unacquainted as I am with the course you are pursuing, and the present state of your enquiries, it may not be out of place to impress upon you the great importance of obtaining a correct statement of the actual amount of bonds in the hands of the public, bearing the West Hartlepool Company's seal of incorporation.

I have strong reasons for claiming your especial attention to this point, and for believing that the books of the Company will not give you the required information.

You will excuse me trespassing upon you with this suggestion, which may probably not be required, but which, I think is only compatible with my duty, to keep prominently before you.

I am, my dear sir, yours faithfully,
(Signed) BENJ. COLEMAN.

Mr. Thos. Sturge,
Northfleet.

London, Sept. 6, 1859.

My dear Sir,—A friend of mine has called my attention to a letter in the *Daily News* of Saturday last on the subject of West Hartlepool affairs, which he naturally thought I had probably written. As this may be the impression of others, I think it necessary to say to you, that I am not the author, and that I have not had anything to do with its production.

In fact, to save the necessity of making further disclaimers should other letters appear on this subject, I repeat to you, that in conformity with your wishes, I will make no move in the matter at present.

I wait most anxiously for your report, which I fully rely on being so comprehensive as to save the necessity of raising my voice, or of writing another word on the affairs of the West Dock Company: in saying this, I of course assume that your report will appear long before the period of the next general meeting of the Company.

I am, my dear Sir, yours faithfully,

(Signed) Benj. Coleman.

Mr. Thos. Sturge,
Northfleet.

Oct. 26, 1859.

My dear Sir,—It is now *eight* months since I placed in your hands the data upon which my charges against the management of the West Dock Company are founded, and for that period I have, at your request, remained perfectly quiescent; I hope, therefore, that you will not consider it premature, nor unreasonable, if I should now press to be informed—confidentially, if you deem it necessary—of the result of your investigations and your views for the future.

If, as I have before said, your report to the share and bond-holders of the West Hartlepool Railway and Dock Company should from any cause fail to confirm my statements, I shall feel it necessary to publicly state my case, which has been materially strengthened by recent information, and thereby protect myself from the certain inference that I have, as Mr. Jackson asserts, made statements which are wholly unfounded.

I hope, however, that I shall, by the completeness of your promised report, be relieved from the necessity of saying another word on the subject of West Hartlepool mismanagement; but I do wish to be assured at once of MY position in the result of this enquiry, that I may without delay decide on my future course of action. I shall be glad to attend to any appointment you may make, and with best respects,

I am, my dear Sir, yours truly,

BENJ. COLEMAN.

Mr. Thos. Sturge.

Northfleet, 31st Oct., 1859.

Dear Sir,—Mr. Sturge requests me to say, that he has just returned from Eastbourne (Friday evening), and that while there and for some weeks before, he has himself been almost exclusively occupied with the Hartlepool affair, and that he hopes in a very few days to be able to appoint a time for meeting you.

I remain, dear Sir, yours truly,

(Signed) GEO. ENDERBY.

B. Coleman, Esq.

London, 5th Nov., 1859.

Dear Sir,—Mr. Sturge will be happy to meet you at Eykyn's, in 'Change Alley, on Monday, 7th instant, at 11 a.m. In great haste.

Yours truly,

(Signed) GEO. ENDERBY.

Bayswater, 48, Pembridge Villas,
Nov. 22, 1859.

My dear Sir,—I have heard that negociations are afloat for the sale of the West Dock Company to a neighbouring line, which if true, is no doubt with your sanction, and I can only hope will be successfully carried through.

But *it may* be a move on the part of Mr. Jackson to gain time, and delay the publicity of your report.

You intended calling a meeting of the committee last week; did it take place, and may I be informed what is the result?*

I will meet you any day you appoint in town, or come down to Northfleet if you prefer it.

I am, my dear Sir, yours faithfully,
(Signed) BENJ. COLEMAN.

Mr. Thos. Sturge.

London, Nov. 23rd, 1859.

My dear Sir,—Some months ago, and *prior* to the General Meeting of the West Hartlepool Dock Company, I travelled in the same carriage from London to York, with Mr. J. E. Coleman, the accountant, and Mr. Ralph Ward Jackson, who made each others' acquaintance on that occasion for the first time.

Mr. Coleman, as you perhaps know, is the official liquidator of the District Bank at Newcastle, which institution had, I believe, dealings with parties connected with West Hartlepool, and the acquaintance thus made seemed mutually interesting.

We all staid at York, and Mr. Coleman intended to travel north with Mr. Jackson on the following morning, but was detained by sudden illness; and in the emergency I was enabled to render him some

* Mr. Sturge had told me at the last interview, when I pressed him to tell me how affairs stood, that he had refused to say anything, even to his colleagues, who knew nothing, and should not until he was ready, when he would call a meeting of the committee, and he thought they would afterwards call a meeting in London of the shareholders.

trifling attention, for which he wrote me a letter of thanks, and expressed his desire to serve me.

At a subsequent interview, on his return to London, and still anterior to the General Meeting, Mr. Coleman told me he had been invited to visit West Hartlepool, and he asked me if he could be of service in the pending dispute. I declined to trouble him, and it so happens, that I have never seen him *since* the Meeting until yesterday, when, to my surprise, he passed me in the street, as if we had been strangers.

Now this altered tone of conduct can only be accounted for by the supposition that he has been prejudiced by impressions received in the north, where I know it is thought that Jackson made a triumphant answer, and had thereby silenced a discomfited libeller. It is therefore of the last importance to me that your report should in a few words embrace my justification. I took it for granted that you would of course do this, in plain and unmistakeable terms; but that you appeared to think, from what you recently said, it would not be necessary.

The incident however to which I allude, and the state of feeling in the north and elsewhere, with reference to me, arising from the silence imposed on me during your investigations, places me at so serious a disadvantage that nothing short of a public justification, either by you or myself, will satisfy me; and as I am not desirous of being again prominent, I hope you and Mr. Bell will think it only fair that it should be done in the report you are about to make to the shareholders. Anxiously waiting which,

I am, my dear Sir, yours truly,
(Signed) Benj. Coleman.

Mr. Thos. Sturge,
Northfleet.

Northfleet, near Gravesend,
2nd Dec., 1859.

* Dear Sir,—Mr. Sturge has desired me to say that

* This letter contains a distinct promise, which Mr. Sturge did not fulfil.

the request made in your last letter will be complied with.

Yours truly,
(Signed) GEO. ENDERBY.

B. Coleman, Esq.,
48, Pembridge Villas.

London, Dec. 14, 1859.

My dear Sir,—Mr. Wilkinson has told me of his interview with you and Mr. Bell, and I now write to request you will be good enough to call on the former when you are next in town, as by a timely understanding all difficulties and cross purposes may be avoided.

I have placed myself in the hands of Messrs. Yarborough & Wilkinson (of 44, Lincoln's Inn Fields), feeling indisposed at this juncture to act on my own responsibility.

My friend, Mr. Wilkinson, is fully acquainted with the case, and my position. His standing in the profession is a guarantee, at the same time, of good faith to your advisers.

I repeat my assurance that my desire is to do nothing prematurely that might defeat any special objects you have in view, but my decided feeling is, that *I ought to know at once* the ground on which I stand, so that Mr. Wilkinson and I may see our way to wait your own time for the publication of your report to the West Hartlepool Proprietors, or to tell you why we cannot.*

I am the more urgent on this point, as there appears in the indefinite observations made by you to me, and by Mr. Bell to Mr. Wilkinson, serious discrepancies;

* Mr. Sturge had told me that the delay in making his report arose from the non-completion of legal documents which would secure a large amount—"many thousands,"—and I must be patient, as any disturbance might frustrate him to the injury of the shareholders.

and I find by my long silence I am placed at a disadvantage no longer endurable.

Mr. Jackson's disingenuous letter addressed to the West Hartlepool Company's proprietors, prior to the last general meeting, and his untruthful statements on that occasion are still uncontradicted, and when it is considered that men, holding the social position of Mr. Bell, endorsed these statements in ignorance, it may be, of facts now known to him, you must see that I at least made a bad bargain in accepting the terms which have kept me silent for ten months, and which have fixed a stigma on my character, inflicting a moral injury, of which I may never know the extent, and from which I may never recover.

It is for these reasons I now press for an explicit statement of what you intend to say to the *shareholders* and I am sure *you* at least, will, under the circumstances, recognise the justice of my request.

I am, my dear Sir, yours faithfully,

(Signed) Benj. Coleman.

Mr. Thos. Sturge, Northfleet.

Northfleet, near Gravesend,
19th December, 1859.

Dear Sir,—In reference to your letter of the 14th instant, Mr. Sturge desires me to say that he has very carefully considered it. He is pleased to learn by it that you have placed yourself in the hands of Yarborough and Wilkinson, of 44, Lincoln's-inn Fields, who he has no doubt will advise you discreetly.

Mr. Sturge thinks that it would be altogether out of place for him to wait on them, as you have in your letter requested him to do, for (among other reasons) should their advice in any respect not meet your views, you might think they had been unduly influenced by him, and because he has nothing whatever to do with your private affairs.

Mr. Sturge only knows you as a shareholder of the West Hartlepool Harbour and Railway, who has avowed that he has no object in view but the success and prosperity of that undertaking. Mr. Sturge's labours are for the same end, and he will continue to pursue that object to the best of his ability.

No one, be he shareholder or director, has any right whatever to ask him, or any member of the Committee, what their report will be before it is given to the directors.

At the proper time the report of the Committee will (Mr. Sturge does not doubt) be published in its entirety.

Mr. Sturge thinks there is no justice in the remarks contained in your letter respecting anything which has been said by him to you, or by himself or Mr. Bell to Mr. Wilkinson. You say in your letter, "You must see that I at least made a bad bargain in accepting the terms which have kept me silent for ten months."

Mr. Sturge entirely denies the existence of any terms or bargain. What he did was only to advise you that it would be better for your own standing to await with patience until the report of the committee should appear, and he thinks so still.

You refer to a letter published by Mr. Jackson. Mr. Sturge only knows Mr. Jackson in his official capacity, and he always has abstained from mixing himself up in any personal matters between yourself and Mr. Jackson. Mr. Sturge's attention has been confined to the affairs of the West Hartlepool Harbour and Railway Company, upon which he has bestowed very great labour.

Mr. Sturge can feel for the suffering you endure from the distracting power of impatience, for he himself is open to this same temptation of the evil one. That it is evil, may be seen in the 2nd Peter, 1st chap. 6th verse, and in Isaiah, 26th chap. 3rd verse, is shewn that peace of mind which results from patience, spoken of by Peter, and how it is to be obtained.

To Mr. Sturge it will be a source of great pleasure,

should what is written be in any degree helpful towards restoring peace to your mind.

I remain, dear Sir, yours truly,
(Signed) GEO. ENDERBY.

B. Coleman, Esq., Pembridge Villas.

Northfleet, near Gravesend, 20 Dec., 1859.

Dear Sir,—I replied to you very fully yesterday on behalf of Mr. Sturge, by which you will see he had made up his mind as to the course the report of the committee must take.

Few things escape Mr. Sturge; I know he was as much surprised as you can be, at seeing the article in the *Railway Times.** I know he will not be influenced by it or anything else that may appear in any shape, but will rest with patience the action of the directors when they get the report, not doubting the result will be good.

I remain, yours truly,
(Signed) GEO. ENDERBY.

B. Coleman, Esq.

December 22, 1859.

Dear Sir,—I duly received Mr. Enderby's letters of the 19th and 20th inst., and I have in consequence of the unexpected nature of the contents of the former, reviewed carefully the correspondence that has taken place between us since our first long and memorable interviews immediately after your return from the last general meeting of the West Hartlepool Harbour and Railway Company, and I can find nothing in it to support the character that is now suddenly sought to be given to our intercourse.

In stating in my previous letters that "I had made a bad bargain" in acceding to a certain understanding,

---

* I had written a short letter calling Mr. Sturge's attention to a remarkable article in the *Railway Times* of December 17th, 1859, commencing "The admirers of judicious enterprise."—*See* Appendix, p. 48.

I used a conventional phrase not meant to be interpreted with pedantic and literal precision, and happily for me, your own letters in my possession confirm that view of the matter, which the expression in question illustrated. The exact words used by you on the second occasion of your calling at my office, when I handed to you my bill of indictment against Mr. Ralph Jackson's management of West Hartlepool Dock Company's matters, were, "Now thee must be quiet, thee must not write another word on the subject at present, I will probe thy statements to the bottom, even if it should cost me the sacrifice of all my interest in the concern," &c., &c.

I considered this an injunction and part of an express understanding, and I have at *a great sacrifice*, kept faith, but fortunately for me, seeing the tone of the letter you have caused to be sent to me, I have done nothing to compromise the position I hold in respect to Mr. Jackson; and the article to which I referred you in the *Railway Times*, shews that, resolute as you are in denying *me* information, other parties at all events, have been more fortunate in obtaining an insight into the nature of the forthcoming report; whether this is just or not, I must leave others to decide.

I am, dear sir, yours truly,
(Signed) BENJ. COLEMAN.

Mr. Thos. Sturge.

December 29, 1859.

My dear Mr. Wilkinson,—I have received the papers, and am obliged by your brief intimation of your interview with Mr. Bell. You do not, however, say that you are promised a copy of Mr. Sturge's report, and as I deem that all important, as a preliminary, I must be excused listening to any advice until we have it, by which we can fairly judge of my future position.

Mr. Sturge's letter of the 19th inst., I look upon as an insult, and his closing homily, exhorting me to practise patience, as an unmerited sneer. His stern denial of my right to ask for information *before it is given to the Directors*, is contrary to what he led me to believe, and is, under the circumstances, most unjust. I am, therefore, preparing for action, and have written to the secretary for a list of the shareholders, to which I hope you see no objection.

I propose calling on you on Saturday morning, when I will explain my views more fully, and at the same time, prove to you by documentary evidence, the statements I made in reference to some of the most remarkable doings at West Hartlepool, which Mr. Sturge does not know—at least he does not know from me.

Yours very truly,
(Signed) BENJ. COLEMAN.

Dec., 29th, 1859.

Sir,—I request to be furnished with a list of the names and *addresses* of the share and bondholders of the West Hartlepool Harbour and Railway Company, for which I am ready to pay the office fees on your informing me the cost of the same.

I was about to press for this information some months ago, but deferred my application, in obedience to the wishes of Mr. Sturge.

I am Sir, your obedt. Servant.
(Signed) BENJ. COLEMAN.

Abraham Basnett, Esq.,
West Hartlepool.

London, Jan. 3, 1860,
28, Threadneedle-street.

Sir,—I wrote on the 29th ult. requesting to be furnished with a list of the shareholders of the West Hartlepool Company, which letter is not acknowledged.

I therefore write again to repeat my request; hoping I may be favoured with a reply by return of post.

Your obedient Servant,
(Signed) BENJ. COLEMAN.

A. Basnett, Esq.

West Hartlepool,
Jan. 7, 1860.

Sir,—I have to acknowledge the receipt of your letter.

Your application has arrived at a time when you will be aware the establishments of every company are more especially engaged in the business of their undertakings preparatory to their general meetings.* Irrespective of this objection to so hurried an addition to the regular work of this Company's staff, at this period of the year, your special reference to Mr. Sturge has induced me to consult my directory, and I am to state to you that under all the circumstances, they consider it only courteous that a communication should be made to that gentleman, which they will take an opportunity of doing.

I am, Sir, your obedient Servant,
(Signed) A. BASNETT, Secretary.

B. Coleman, Esq.,
28, Threadneedle-street,
London, *E. C.*

London, Jan. 25, 1860.

Dear Sir,—I write to ask the favour of an interview with you—if it be quite agreeable—when you are next in town.

I have certainly felt aggrieved, whether justly so or not, at the altered tone you have adopted towards me since the close of your enquiries into the matters of West Hartlepool, and in the absence of knowing what

---

* The same excuse was made last year, when I applied for a list of the shareholders.

course you intend to pursue—whether I shall be compromised in any degree, or entirely exonerated by your report, or whether it is to be withheld from me and the shareholders, until the day of the next general meeting I am necessarily obliged to prepare for the worst. But before I take an irretrievable step, I have thought it only right to ask you to meet me, by which you may avert the necessity of my proceeding in the course I have resolved on and thus save a great deal of vexation and misery to more than one of the many parties involved in this remarkable enquiry.

In the *Railway Times* of December 31st, there appeared a most abusive *leading* article written on the assumption that I was the writer of a recent letter to the *Daily News.* I did not know of the existence of either until some days after, when I wrote to disclaim any knowledge whatever of the authorship, and I repeated what I have said to you,—that I have never written one word to the Press on the subject of West Hartlepool, since the last general meeting of the Company.

But you must see, that being constantly subject, as I have been to these attacks—unwise and unscrupulous as they are—I am placed at a great disadvantage by the silence you recommended, and I agreed to adopt. I am, however, now in a position to roll back this accumulated mass of falsehood and scoundrelism, and deprived of all fair consideration, as it appears to me, I hope to stand justified in the eyes of the world for the course I may feel compelled hereafter to pursue.

I am, dear Sir, yours truly,

(Signed) BENJ. COLEMAN.

Mr. Thos. Sturge.

Northfleet, near Gravesend,
30 Jany., 1860.

Dear Sir,—After you had told Mr. Sturge that you had placed your affairs in the hands of your solicitors, he thinks you ought not to have written to him your letter of the 14th December, 1859, asking him to wait on your solicitors, and implying a threat, assuming rights which you do not possess together with remarks not fair to him.

Mr. Sturge thinks your solicitors never saw that letter from you to him, or they would have at once seen the necessity that your letter should be properly answered in the manner in which it was answered. That reply to your letter was written in all sincerity without any design to offend you.

Mr. Sturge was very sorry to see the comments in the *Railway Times*, on some letter of which you complain, he never for a moment believed that you were in any way concerned in the letter, and he was glad to see the promptness with which the mistake was corrected.

Mr. Sturge is, and will be for several days to come, fully occupied with important business.

Mr. Sturge will give your request of the 25th, for an interview, due consideration. If he consent, it will only be with a view of satisfying you that a paragraph in the report of the committee of assistance, is just to you; but he says, after what has passed, if he does meet you, it must be in the presence of third parties, to prevent misconceptions and misconstructions of what may be said. As soon as he has decided one way or the other, you will be informed.

I remain, yours truly,
(Signed) GEO. ENDERBY.

B. Coleman, Esq.

London, Jan. 31, 1860.

Dear Sir,—I have received Mr. Enderby's letter of the 30th inst , and having no wish to be misunderstood, I beg to explain that any implied threats which you seem to have discovered in my letters, could have no application, under any circumstances, to you personally.

I think, however, the tone of my letters has been

one of *complaint* rather than threat; I have appealed to you for relief to save, by a timely understanding, all unnecessary complications, and thus to relieve me from the necessity of taking steps for my own vindication.

With the recollection of the antecedent circumstances, you can hardly feel surprised that, remaining quiet with the assurance that, for prudential motives you could not, for a time, say more than that I should be "justified." I should feel discontented and disappointed to find when your report on the affairs of the West Dock Company was completed, you had given it to the *directors*—the men inculpated—instead of shewing it first to the members of the *nominal* committee, and then to have presented it to the shareholders at a special meeting, as I understood you intended to do; and that now on the eve of a general meeting of the Company, the only person who appears to have a knowledge of the report, is the chairman, who avails himself of that advantage, to work the Press in the most daring manner, an article plainly from his pen, whilst admitting that the committee have discovered "that dividends have been improperly paid"—"that mistakes in calculation have not been avoided"—and "that the capital has been exceeded by about £500,000!" Nevertheless, "Rejoices at the appointment of the committee, and the recognition which must be made of the directors' services!!"

This unblushing impudence is followed by a general misleading summary of the Bill of Indemnity now before Parliament, which admits that it is not £500,000 that is deficient, but more than £1,000,000! and then a leading article in the *Railway Times* abuses me by name on an entirely groundless charge, and a hope is expressed that I should not "be too eager to discover another 'mare's nest.'"

With all this, in addition to the serious disadvantages which I have suffered by my silence during the eleven months of your investigation, is it not natural that I should be anxious to know how *I* have been dealt with in your report? that I might not on the one hand do anything unfair or premature, nor on the other lose the opportunity of vindicating myself, by proving the truth of all I have ever charged against the management of the West Hartlepool Dock and Railway Company.

Trusting that you will fix an early day for our interview, which I suggest should be in the presence of Mr. Bell and Mr. Wilkinson,

I am, dear Sir, yours truly,
(Signed) Benj. Coleman.

Mr. Thos. Sturge, Northfleet.

Northfleet, near Gravesend,
2nd Feb., 1860.

Dear Sir,—On the 30th January I wrote, that as soon as Mr. Sturge had decided upon your application for a personal interview, you would be apprised.

I have now to say, that on due consideration Mr. Sturge feels that he has no authority to communicate any part of the report made to the directors.

To satisfy your mind, he has already told you that the report contains a paragraph just to you, therefore you must remain satisfied with that assurance for the present; this gives him the less concern, because it will not be long before the report will be published in its entirety.

There is one thing I can tell you, which you may be glad to hear: it is, that the funds of the Company have not been used to promote the personal interest of any director. As Mr. Sturge can say nothing more to the purpose, you will excuse him for not complying with your request, as he must now give attention to his own affairs, which will fully occupy him till the next meeting of the Company.

I remain, yours truly,
(Signed) Geo. Enderby.

Benj. Coleman, Esq.,
48, Pembridge Villas, Bayswater.

London, Feb. 3, 1860.

Dear Sir,—I am much obliged by the receipt of Mr. Enderby's letter of the 2nd instant, and regret that you do not think you are justified in saying more on the report than that it will contain a paragraph exonerating me, and that as it is shortly to be published in its entirety, you think the interview I have asked for unnecessary.

I am also told, "that the funds of the Company have not been used to promote the personal interest of any director."

May I intrude upon you so far as to ask two questions?

> *First.* Am I to understand that the report will be made public a reasonable length of time before the next general meeting of the Company?
>
> *And Secondly.* Am I to understand that the funds and credit of the West Hartlepool Dock and Railway Company have not been improperly used at any time for the purchase and support of steam boats and collieries unconnected with the Company, but in which the chairman, Mr. R. W. Jackson, held a very large interest?

Mr. Jackson has stated that this, among other charges, is wholly unfounded; and it would indeed be gratifying, as you say, to me, to learn that I have done him injustice in harbouring such a suspicion.

Not doubting that your report will be a full and perfectly fair document,

I am, dear Sir, yours truly,
(Signed) BENJ. COLEMAN.

Mr. Thos. Sturge, Northfleet.

Northfleet, near Gravesend,
Feb. 6, 1860.

Dear Sir,—Mine to you of the 2nd February, ended all Mr. Sturge will say before the meeting.

I remain your obedient Servant,
(Signed) GEO. ENDERBY.

B. Coleman, Esq., Bayswater.

Feb. 27, 1860.

Dear Sir,—You are one of the last men whom the commercial world would suspect of being easily deceived, or who would fail to fulfil any trust confided to your care and management; I am therefore at a loss to account for the course you have pursued in the affairs of West Hartlepool, and I am forced to ask of you respectfully an explanation of the cause of your absenting yourself from the general meeting of the Company, and of the real intent and meaning of the report made by "The Committee of Consultation," which is published and bears your signature as chairman, as I think I am placed by that report in an unfair and false position.

To clear the ground, and to avoid any misapprehension, I beg to recal to your memory the circumstances under which I was induced to place in your hands the facts upon which I had grounded my charges against Mr. R. W. Jackson, and the general management of the Company, over which he presides.

Awakened by the gravity of my remarks at the general meeting of 1859, you came self-invited to my office to know the meaning of the statements I had made; and after receiving from me the most unreserved explanations, you undertook to make a searching investigation into West Hartlepool affairs, and for this purpose I handed to you on your second visit to my office, a book in which I had written up for your guidance and instruction, the chief points of my allegations; you then recommended me not to interfere in any way for the present; you said you had a perfect knowledge of the Company's affairs from their origin; you had negotiated the sale of the Clarence Railway with Mr. Jackson, and had great influence over him. The best course for me to pursue would be to remain silent, and not to write anything more until you had made yourself master of the facts; I consented to do so, expressing myself well pleased that the case would be in such able hands. And you have since expressed yourself satisfied that I have faithfully kept my promise.

About this period (March, 1859) there appeared a series of articles in the leading columns of the *Durham Advertiser*, *Hartlepool Mercury*, *Mining Journal* and *Railway Times*, imputing to me the worst conduct in reference to Mr. Jackson, stigmatizing me as a libeller, whose unfounded aspersions had been scattered to the winds.

I pointed your attention to these articles which were plainly inspired by Mr. Jackson, and I have frequently since complained to you of the serious disadvantages I laboured under by the silence imposed upon me, and you have as frequently advised me not to notice them, and to be patient, particularly as the result would be satisfactory to me. You said at different times, "You will be justified"—"No reflection will rest upon you"—"You will be pleased to learn that the man whose mind had been the most strongly prejudiced against you (Mr. Alfred Bell) had completely changed his opinion, and had said, 'Not another word must be said against Coleman,'" &c. &c. I refer you to our several interviews, and to your own letters commencing on the 10th March, 1859. I particularly claim your attention to my letter of November 23rd, and to your reply. After complaining of the further greivance I was suffering, from the prolonged delay in the production of your report, I said, "It is therefore of the last importance to me, that your report should in a few words embrace my justification."—"The state of feeling in the north and elsewhere, with reference to me, arising from the silence imposed on me during your investigations, places me at so serious a disadvantage, that nothing short of a public justification either by you or myself will satisfy me; and as I am not desirous of being again prominent, I hope you and Mr. Bell will think it only fair that it should be done in the report you are about to make to the shareholders."

To the letter I received the following reply, dated December 2nd, 1859:—

Dear Sir,—Mr. Sturge has desired me to say, that

the request you made in your last shall be complied with.

Yours truly,

GEO. ENDERBY.

With this distinct assurance, though suffering much in my commercial position, from the continued misrepreutations in the papers under Mr. Jackson's influence, I made up my mind to wait as patiently as I could for the appearance of your report, being confident from my own undoubted knowledge of the facts, that if it dealt with them at all, it must contain a complete corroboration of the worst charges I have ever made against the financial position and general management of the West Hartlepool Harbour and Railway Company; and I remained the more readily quiet at that moment, from your assuring me that the delay had arisen from the non-completion of legal documents, which would secure to the Company a very large amount of property, and any premature disclosures might disturb the arrangement to the detriment of the stock and bondholders' interests, "my own holding," you said, "being exclusively in the first preference shares of the Company, is not affected; my exertions are, therefore, quite disinterested, and for the benefit of others."

My discontent at not being permitted to see the report, and surprise at your decision at last to hand it (contrary I think to your first intention,) to the directors, has been already expressed to you; but I was in no way—I could not be—prepared after all that has passed between us, to find that the report read at the general meeting, should be entirely silent on the questions I have raised, and that my justification, according to your promise, is not mentioned. I am named, it is true, in a manner so perfectly Jacksonian, that if the wording of the paragraph be not Mr. Ralph Jackson's own, it is doubtless Mr. Bell's, whose long and intimate association with his friend and patron, has led him to adopt a close imitation of that style of negative truth, for which Mr. Jackson is distinguished. The same observation will apply to the bill before

Parliament, which, I am told, is most disingenuously and craftily worded.*

All attempts on my part to obtain any decided answers to my questions put to the chairman at the meeting, on the subject of the report and the Bill, were unavailing; he affected not to know its leading features, and discovered at length, that the copy, I and another proprietor present had in our hands, and obtained of course from the Company's agents, were not the same as he was reading from, it having been altered, he said, since its first introduction.

Mr. Nicholas Wood, as well as Mr. Jackson, having referred me to you for information, I am about to trouble you with a few questions, and beg to ask—

1*st.* Did you in the course of your enquiries find the Company sound and prosperous?

2*nd.* Where the Company's accounts kept with ordinary correctness and fidelity?

3*rd.* Have bonds of an irregular character ever been issued, and if so, by whose sanction, and for what purpose?

4*th.* Have bonds at any time been issued in excess of the Company's powers?

5*th.* Did you find that the collieries and steam boats were the property and *had beeu so for several years*, of the Company, or were they the property of Mr. Jackson and others?

6*th.* Has the Company's credit in bonds aud bills ever been used for the purchase and maintenance of these steam-boats and collieries?

7*th.* What property did Mr. Jackson and others make over to you, and for what object?

8*th.* Did you not discover *a large* deficiency, and obtained all the private property you could to cover it?

9*th.* Is there not at least half a million more or less deficient, and is not the Bill before Parliament

* It will be seen in sequel that this Bill was withdrawn in consequence of my intended opposition. *See* Appendix.

intended to cover past transactions, and in fact a "Bill of Indemnity?"

10*th*. Have dividends ever been paid out of capital?

11*th*. Will not the effect of the bill be, if passed, to lessen the value of the *legitimately* issued bonds and stock?

12*th*. Whether the bill passes or not, will it make any difference in the real value of the first preference shares, such as you hold exclusively?*

13*th*. Have you ever asked me to prove any of my allegations, or are you aware of any one of the Committee having done so?

14*th* and lastly. Are my charges in your opinion substantially correct, or are they not?

In conclusion, I beg to inform you that finding the report of the committee of consultation, instead of "justifying" me, conveyed the idea that having condoned my errors, they were disposed to forgive me in consideration of the benefits I had accidently conferred on the Company, I made in the face of the meeting these observations.

"I now charge the chairman, Mr. Ralph Ward Jackson, with having issued bonds of an irregular character, which, as soon as they were questioned, he hastily withdrew by sending his cheque for the amount; and *I dare* the chairman or any one of his supporters to put me to the proof of that transaction."

I need not say that if *you* are in a position to negative my assertions on this head or any other of the serious charges I have made against Mr. Jackson, you ought in mercy to him to do it, and if you are not, you are bound as a man of honour to relieve me from the serious imputations which he and his supporters have cast upon me, by saying that from vindictive motives I have made statements to his and the Company's prejudice, which have no foundation in fact.

* The preference shares in this Company have priority over the debentures.

Awaiting the favour of an early reply, and informing you that a meeting of the share and bondholders is convened at the London Tavern, for twelve o'clock on Thursday next, at which I hope you will attend.

I am, dear sir, your obedient servant,
(Signed) BENJ. COLEMAN.

Mr. Thos. Sturge, Northfleet.

Northfleet, near Gravesend,
28th Feb., 1860.

Sir,—A letter of three sheets from you to Mr. Sturge, dated 27th February, 1860, is merely noticed to say that Mr. Sturge does not admit the correctness of what you say, and that it is offensive in its character, and one that ought not to have been written by you.

It would be a useless waste of time to attempt to remove your unjust suspicions and conclusions, or to attempt to prove to you that black is black, and white is white.

Mr. Sturge's work is finished, and he is perfectly satisfied that all that he has done is for the interest of all concerned in the affairs of the West Hartlepool Harbour and Railway Company; let your opinion be what it may, it is not for him to trouble himself about it.

He has completed his labours, and you are to understand that he will have no further correspondence with you.

I remain, your most obedient servant,
GEO. ENDERBY.

Benj. Coleman, Esq.,
Pembridge Villas.

London, Feb. 29, 1860.

Sir,—I am in receipt of Mr. Enderby's letter of yesterday's date, and I regret to find you do not admit the correctness of what I say.

This is a denial in terms too general to be grappled with, and therefore I must rely upon our correspondence, which I hope and think, will substantially support all the statements made in my letter of the 27th inst.

You think "it would be a useless waste of time to attempt to remove my unjust suspicions;" which of them? Are all unjust? Is it unjust to say that Mr. Jackson has dealt with the bonds of the West Hartlepool Company in an improper and irregular manner? Is it incorrect to say that you knew that this was one of my charges which you pledged your word to enquire into, and that you have never asked me to prove?

Would it be a useless waste of time to relieve Mr. Jackson from this and other imputations which I have made, and which he and his supporters say are vindictive libels?

You and your professional adviser, Mr. Alfred Bell, have the reputations of being men of high honor, stern integrity, and above all—Christian character!

You are therefore the last men to flinch from the the discharge of a solemn duty at whatever cost, and are bound, I think, to restore Mr. Jackson or myself to the good opinion of society, by saying whether you find my charges against him—true or false?

I am, Sir, your obedient servant,

BENJ. COLEMAN.

Mr. Thos. Sturge.

APPENDIX.

WEST HARTLEPOOL HARBOUR AND RAILWAY COMPANY.

Report of Proceedings at a Public Meeting, held at the London Tavern, on Thursday, March 1st, 1860. W. M. WILKINSON, *Esq., in the Chair.*

A Meeting of Debenture and Shareholders in the West Hartlepool Harbour and Railway Company, was held on Thursday, March 1st, at the London Tavern, "To consider the provisions of the Company's Bill now in Parliament, which seriously prejudices their claims in the Company, and to take measures to protect their interests before Parliament." The chair was occupied by W. M. Wilkinson, Esq.

THE CHAIRMAN in opening the proceedings, said: Gentlemen, I wish to give you shortly the reason why I have adopted this somewhat extraordinary course of asking you, whether you are aware of the position in which the bondholders and shareholders of this Company stand with reference to what is proposed by the Bill now before the Committee of the House of Commons. The meeting is called "To consider the provisions of the Company's Bill now in Parliament, which seriously prejudices their claims on the Company, and to take measures to protect their interests before Parliament." Now, my name is Wilkinson, of the firm of Yarborough and Wilkinson, of 44, Lincoln's Inn Fields, and I have, along with another gentleman who is trusteee with me, been for some years the proprietor of bonds in this Company, which now amount by subsequent purchases, to £4,500. I merely mention that, because some person, I suppose the secretary, in the interests of the Company, has thought it worth while to insert this in an advertisement which appears in the London papers. "In advertising the resolutions that were passed at a general meeting at Hartlepool, the other day, I am instructed to request the insertion of the following resolutions unamiously passed at a special general meeting of the Company, held on the 23rd instant; and I am at the same time instructed to state that Messrs. Yarborough and Wilkinson, whose signatures are attached to an advertisement convening a meeting in London, on the 1st of March, are the solicitors of Mr. Benjamin Coleman, who holds only £100 stock in the Company." I do not myself think, speaking to London merchants and gentlemen, that it is of any very great consequence whether I represent a pers·n who holds £100 stock or £100,000; the main question is, whether what I say is true, or not, and whether it is sufficiently interesting to the shareholders to justify me in taking the step of bringing them together upon this occasion. This, however, is a very disingenuous statement, and it is no doubt intended to prejudice me before you. Mr. Jackson and the solicitors of the Company are perfectly well aware, and have been for some months from my own mouth, that I am interested to the extent I have mentioned, as a debenture holder. Now you are all aware that debenture holders have not the right to attend the meetings of railway companies; that is, because we are supposed to have a preference in the payment of our interest and principal. We are in fact, mortgagees of the Company. Now to start with, and to show that possibly some of you may be in error as to that fact, let me say that I have been at the trouble of looking through the Acts of Parliament of this Company, and I find that according to the Act of 1852, under which the largest portion of the debentures are issued, the bondholders are deferred to all the preference shareholders. We are not in the ordinary position of bondholders in other companies, but we are deferred to the preference shareholders, and that accounts to some extent in my mind, for some of the recommendations which are made in this Bill now before Parliament, by the committee which has been sitting for some twelve months, to investigate these affairs. the members of which happen to be interested as preference shareholders, and therefore may not be supposed to have the interests of bondholders very prominently kept before their eyes. However, that of itself would not be a sufficient excuse for my giving you the trouble of coming here to-day, but my other reasons for doing it are these: At the meeting in February, 1859, now twelve months ago, there were certain questions asked. There had been a correspondence previously published, both by Mr. Coleman, and by Mr. Jackson, the Chairman. That on the part of Mr. Coleman making some very serious charges against Mr. Jackson, of having been for many years a large colliery and steam-boat owner, and having subsidized himself out of the proceeds of the Company's funds. Whatever truth there may be in that statement will remain to be seen hereafter, and it is one which, if it be true, is of considerable importance to the shareholders. But whether it be true or not, that accusation was made. I now understand from having become more acquainted with these matters and having had communications with many gentlemen on the subject, both by letter and personally, that there have been for many years, ideas prevalent in the neighbourhood, that all was not quite so fair and above-board as has been represented at the Company's meetings. Mr. Jackson, not so many years ago, was a humble attorney like myself, of Stockton; now he is a great man living at Greatham Hall, and having apparently an unlimited command of means; so much so as that he is the registered owner, sole or in part, of ten collieries in the West Hartlepool district. I do not know exactly what position he has taken up with reference to the steamboat service trading from West Hartlepool to St. Petersburgh and Copenhagen, to Hamburgh and to Rotterdam; at all events he has had a considerable connection with them, and rumour attributes to him either the whole, or the larger part, of the interest in that concern. I cannot say whether that be true or not, therefore I do not wish to make any absolute statement that it is so. With reference to the charge that was made by Mr. Coleman against Mr. Jackson previous to the meeting in February, 1859, Mr. Jackson denied it in words which I am now about to read to you, and you will see what, as common-sense persons, your understanding of these words is, and would have been, at the time if you had read them:—"I have to state to you that the West Hartlepool Company do not possess, directly or indirectly, one inch of coal property in the kingdom, and that they have no responsibility or connection whatever with the working of any such property; neither have I or any other director, ever derived from, or asked the Company to benefit anyone of us by any means of that sort, either as respects collieries, steamboats, or any other description of property whatever." Now, I think if I had made a charge against Mr. Jackson, or any one else, of having been subsidizing himself out of the funds of a company of which he was the chairman, I should have been perfectly satisfied with this refutation of my charge; and supposing that upon enquiry it turned out that his statement was correct, I should most humbly make every apology to him for having brought a false accusation against him. Now, having laid that little foundation to which I beg your particular attention, because it will be found of importance in the subsequent observations, which I have to address to you, I will only proceed to say that those charges, having been made in so public a manner before the meeting, it was thought, very justly and creditably to the directors, that the only way of meeting such a charge as this, was to have a committee of enquiry. There have been many circumstances connected with the Company which have created great suspicions at different times; and amongst other things certainly not the least suspicious has been the constitution of the directory itself. I do not know to what extent you, gentlemen, may be aware of the circumstances of the directory, as I do not know whom I have the honour to address. I have no doubt that you are aware that Mr. Ralph Ward Jackson is the chairman, and has been so for many years. The next director is Mr. Chales Ward Jackson, who is his son. I do not know his exact age, but I believe it is about five, or six, or seven and twenty. Another director is Mr. Swainston, of Preston, which is about 200 miles from West Hartlepool, a gentleman who is Mr. Jackson's father-in-law, and is 80 years old. The fourth director is Mr. Robinson Watson, a woollen draper at Stockton, some little distance from Hartlepool; and the remaining director, the fifth, (there being five directors required as a minimum by the Act of Parliament) is Mr. Cuthbert Wigham, a gentleman who is very infirm, and, moreover, blind. These are the gentlemen who have the management of our concern. If you are perfectly satisfied with this, I had better say at once that I am not. I am not satisfied with it at the first blush, considering that five is the minimum; and that just previous to the meeting in February, 1859, when the first indications of unpleasantness arose, there was a secession from the board of two directors, and two others had previously, I understand, seceded. Now, that being the case, I do not wonder that it should be felt by these five gentlemen that it would be, in the face of such charges as had been made, very desirable indeed that there should be an independent committee to investigate the circumstances which had been alleged with reference to the dealings with the Company's funds, though I may say those were not the absolute terms in which the matter was referred to this committee of investigation. The terms as I take them from the published Report given at the last year's meeting are these:—"To assist them with their advice as to the best mode of disposing of the surplus property of the Company, and to co-operate with them generally in the interests of the Company." Those were the terms in which the gentlemen were appointed. There was a great deal of laudation about the state of the Company's accounts, and apparently, I am bound to say that they were very satisfactory, inasmuch as the accounts showed that of the capital of £2,686,000, £335,000 was "unexhausted"—that is the word used—"leaving unexhausted" (which means not called up, I suppose.) "a sum of £335,000." A dividend of 4 per cent. was paid, and everything seemed perfectly satisfactory. In the summary of the accounts of that meeting, there was given an item which is one of the principal items to which I now wish to draw your attention. And let me say here, in this early stage of the business, that I am really asking for information myself in a great measure. What I have before me are the published accounts of the directors for the last two years, and the report of Mr. Sturge and Committee of Assistance, together with the Bill in Parliament which I hold in my hand; and it is from these sources only that I draw the information upon which I am founding the observations that I now make to you. In this account, which is so satisfactory, there is an item in the summary of the general balance sheet—"Balance of current account, £21,775 16*s.* 4*d.*" Now to show you the necessity of bearing that in mind, I will give you the corresponding item in the account which was read on the 23rd of last month—this day week—"Balance of accounts and securities owing to and by the Company, £578,109 9*s.* 4*d.*, showing a rise of a very considerable amount." Now, that item appears to me one that is worth our while to look into. There is no explanation of it given in the accounts whatever. The accounts for the meeting in February, 1859, are audited by Messrs. Baynes and Fossick, "Audited and found correct.—We have also examined the share register, which we also find correct.—George Baynes, William Fossick, auditors." And this correct account contains the balance of current accounts, amounting to £21,000, which is increased at the next meeting by £550,000, without any explanation whatever being given. The same gentlemen's names are appended to the account containing this larger item as before—"Audited and found correct, George Baynes, William Fossick." Now there is no information whatever given to us as to the large and sudden increase of those figures. It was stated at the meeting in 1859 that there was this unexhausted capital of £335,000, and that the unexhausted portion had been reduced; that there had been a fresh issue of capital reducing it to £149,000 at the last meeting. Now, if you please, I will bring you back to the circumstances connected with the appointment of the sub-committee—charges having been made impugning the correctness of the Company's accounts—that obviously became the first matter for those gentlemen to enquire into. It was rather a heterogeneous committee—by the way, this committee of consultation, or investigation, or whatever it may be called, I do not remember all their names, but I believe it consisted of Mr. Thomas Sturge, of Northfleet; Admiral Cator, who lives in London; Mr. Birley, of Preston; Mr. Baynes, the auditor; and Mr. Nicholas Wood, who resides in the county of Durham, who has himself large dealings with the Company.

A Shareholder.—How many of these gentlemen acted upon that committee? I think several resigned.

The Chairman.—I am going to tell you. One of the gentlemen was nominated at the meeting, obviously without any previous consent on his part, for he resigned before the meeting was over, or before he left the town. The other persons were all scattered about.

A Shareholder.—Give us the name.

The Chairman.—Mr. Birley resigned. Now I do not know whether you are in the habit of employing admirals as accountants, but I should think they were not the best persons in the world. It so happened however that of those gentlemen who were nominated upon the committee of assistance, not one of them has acted substantially, except Mr. Thomas Sturge—a gentleman of between 70 and 80. He told me his age only a few weeks ago, but I forgot it. Cetainly one would have thought that he was the most unlikely person to have bothered himself with such an investigation as it afterwards turned out was so absolutely necessary to be made. But I believe there is a Providence in these matters, as well as in every other with which we are concerned, and it turned out that Mr. Sturge was struck by some of the observations that were made by Mr. Coleman at the meeting, in February, 1859; he thought about them, and after revolving the matter in his mind, and not being perfectly satisfied, I suppose, with all the explanations that were made by Mr. Jackson, he made an appointment to meet Mr. Coleman on his return to London, and at that meeting, which lasted for five hours, Mr. Coleman laid before him what he tells me he calls his bill of indictment, containing the various charges that have been made, the rumours and the information he had got in many ways as to the wide-spread idea prevailing that Mr. Jackson's collieries and steamboats were supported in some manner out of the funds of the Company, and that there had been an over-issue of bonds—in other words, that for his private purposes the bonds of the Company had been used to support these speculations of his own. Those were the charges, whether true or false, it is not for me to say, and I do not intend to say. I am only drawing inferences arising from the published documents which I have before me of the Company itself.

A Shareholder.—May I ask if Mr. Coleman is present?

The Chairman.—Yes; he is present. Mr. Sturge, in consequence of this meeting with Mr. Coleman, had another meeting, which lasted for several hours; after which he said, "I will investigate these affairs to the very bottom, if it costs me the whole of my holding in this Company. I and my family hold £50,000 in the Preference Stock of the Company, and if it costs me the whole of the money, I will investigate the charges that you have made." Nothing could be more proper than that, or apparently more beneficial to the Company. Mr. Sturge telegraphed to Mr. Jackson, and told him that that was his determination. Mr. Jackson came up and said he was very glad to hear it; that he was very glad to hear that there was to be this searching investigation into the Company's affairs. Mr. Sturge at once ordered up the clerks of the Company, and all the Company's books to Northfleet, near Gravesend, where he had them for many weeks; and I believe he did give the books a complete turning over. It was not the ordinary auditing of accounts, which we are all acquainted with in public companies—"Audited and found correct, A. B. and C. D."—which I believe those who are interested in large public companies know is not generally worth the paper that it is written upon. But I believe Mr. Sturge audited these accounts, and that he does at this moment know the very bottom of them—the head and tail, and every matter connected with the accounts of the Company. It was not many weeks after he had made this investigation before he made a discovery, which he communicated to Mr. Coleman—in ambiguous terms certainly; but he gave him most clearly to understand that there were very serious defalcations in the accounts. Mr. Coleman having many friends who were interested as bondholders in the concern was naturally anxious to know more of the matter—to know really something about the point that has brought you here to-day. For I suppose, you thought that as there was an advertisement calling you together, it might possibly affect your pockets, and that is why you have come here to-day. Mr. Coleman, having a similar feeling, went direct to the point, and he asked Mr. Sturge what was the prospect for the bondholders. Mr. Sturge, who is well acquainted with commercial affairs, said, "Well, at all events I am safe, and I think the bondholders are safe to a very considerable extent, possibly three-fourths, or something of that sort."

Mr. Baker.—How three-fourths, and not the whole?

The Chairman.—Why, I suppose, that on a valuation, so far as it had proceeded, of the Company's affairs, as he did not see his way (since the preference shareholders came before the debenture holders)—he did not see his way with absolute certainty to the payment of the bondholders in full. That was his idea.

Mr. Baker.—I wish to ask you how far the preference shares go. I think they have only power to raise a certain amount.

The Chairman.—That I cannot tell you, But it is a very pertinent question indeed, and one that I hope the result of this day's proceedings will elicit an answer to. There are gentlemen here who were present at the meeting and took part in it, and I hope they will be able to give us information upon that point. At present we have none beyond what I shall call your attention to. I can tell you what the sum is that the Company is authorized to borrow upon debentures. The amount is £671,000; and at the meeting in 1859 the debenture holding was stated at £650,000. Between that time and this it has been made up to £671,521, which is the full amount of the Company's powers.

Mr. Baker.—The question I wish to ask is, how far they had the power to give the preference shares a priority over the mortgage bonds.

The Chairman.—They have no power but what is given by the Act of Parliament I hold in my hand, which was passed in 1852; at the 96th section you will find——

Mr. Baker.—Allow me to call in question the position that you took up—that the preference shares are prior to the debentary bonds.

The Chairman.—I shall be very glad to find that you are right, for my own personal interests. But still as this is a meeting of shareholders of all classes in the Company, it is a question that does not so immediately press for an answer, as far as the general interests of the Company are concerned, which I desire as much as possible to keep in view, and not merely to regard the interests of those who are simply bondholders.

Mr. Baker.—I thought this was a meeting of bondholders?

The Chairman.—It is a meeting of bond and shareholders. Now I have gone into the circumstances attending the early part of this report; and I have told you that, according to Mr. Sturge's statements, there were some very serious discoveries made.

Mr. Powell.—Have you got this in writing; or is this the remembrance of a conversation?

The Chairman.—This is the remembrance of a conversation, coupled with acts and matters which are in writing. I shall be very glad to give you both. I shall be glad to give you the writing so far as it extends; but it is well to supplement it by something else, in order that you may understand the position. Now you will bear in mind the remarks that Mr. Jackson published previous to the meeting:—"That the Company do not possess, directly or indirectly, one inch of coal property in the kingdom;—that they have no responsibility or connection with the working of any such property." Now I tried very hard to get to know from Mr. Sturge what this report of the committee was to be, because I was told both by him and Mr. Bell, the solicitor to the Company, that the report of the committee was prepared some months ago—two months, perhaps, before it was delivered—and that it was intended to be delivered to the directors; against which I remonstrated if it was of such a nature as to cast any reflection upon the directors. It appeared to me to be not quite a proper thing that a committee should be appointed to supervise the acts of the directors; and then if they should find something strange in the accounts, that they should regard the directors as the proper persons to receive this report. I should tell you that it was impossible for me to get any idea as to what the report was, except that it was stated to me, both by Mr. Bell and Mr. Sturge, that the collieries were found to be much more valuable than had been expected, in consequence of there having been a discovery of a large bed of coal very recently, of which a sample had been sent to London and found to be very good. Knowing that it had been stated that the Company was not interested in any of the collieries, this struck me as rather a remarkable reason to give me for gratulation as to the state of the Company's affairs, and I said to Mr. Bell, "What has the Company to do with it? Because you have said that the Company has no interest whatever in any of the collieries." And he said, "Neither has it. It has no interest whatever." I should tell you that in none of the published accounts of the Company is there one single farthing put down in the way of subsidy, or otherwise to any collieries, or to any steam-boat speculations of any kind. There is no trace of it whatever to be found in the Company's reports. I was startled however from the state into which I was lulled by Mr. Bell's statement as to the prospects of the Company being so good, by an article which appeared in the *Railway Times*, and which is the only document not published by the directors, to which I wish to call your attention. It begins in rather a strange way; and it deals with a document, apparently emanating from this committee of assistance. I am now reading from the *Railway Times*, of the 17th of December last:—"*The admirers of judicious enterprise* will be glad to learn that the committe of consultation, in March last, have nearly completed their labours, and that the report to be furnished by them will be of a most satisfactory character, *even should the immediate remedy be of a sharp description.* They have not contented themselves with mere examination of books, or inspection of vouchers. They have, by competent agents, viewed the dock accommodation, as well as ascertained its cost; *appraised the steamers* as well as other working-stock; and *scrutinized the collieries*, both as to their apparent and latent wealth. *Discrepancies in the accounts have not merely been detected* and traced, but the whole financial position of the Company has been investigated, and *capital and revenue placed upon an equitable basis. The capital*, if we mistake not, will be found to have been *exceeded by about* £500,000; but assets of adequate value exist to account for the whole of the outlay. The Bill of which notice has been given will establish and regulate these matters beyond further misconception or distrust. It has also been ascertained, we believe, that *various losses in revenue have not been kept prominently in view*, and consequently that *dividend has been paid to some extent on earnings not received. These discrepancies will be brought out by the committee*, not with the object of attaching delinquency where none exists, but simply to show that errors in judgment, and mistakes in calculation, have not been altogether avoided. The property itself is in sound, healthy, and regularly improving condition. The trade of the port evinces a solidity and progress as gratifying as it is surprising, whilst the interest of the Company in its docks, steamers, and collieries is proved to be of even greater promise *than had been anticipated. Some revelations in regard to the collieries*, we understand, will be of a description which will more than justify the prudence of having attached them to the Company, while their future working and development, on the other hand, is likely to be made the subject of a special recommendation." Now I thought this was very strange, after what we had been told.

Mr. Taylor: With regard to the case of paying dividends out of unreceived earnings, I think that is perfectly just. It is done in most companies. It is very intelligible. The revenue has been earned, and has been taken perhaps as a good debt.

The Chairman: If that were the case in this document, and which is put forward evidently by some person whose interest it is to make the report of the committee appear as favourable as possible to the directors, he would not have selected that as one of the matters which he had to gloss over—it may or may not be a proper thing. However, having read this article, I took it in my hand to the solicitors of the Company, and complained of the purport of the report being allowed to come out to other persons, when it was not given to those who were the most interested in it, and I wished to know whether it was with their knowledge or that of Mr. Sturge, or by their desire that such a statement as this of the nature of the report was made. Mr. Bell told me that he highly disapproved of putting such a gloss as this upon it; that he could not understand how the nature of this report had oozed out, unless it was through the misdealing of his law stationer or some person entrusted with it. Now you will bear in mind the nature of this article; it points to discrepancies in the accounts, to the payment, as I read it, of dividends out of capital, and to the Company having been obliged to take suddenly to some collieries and steamboats; and it is now found by the report which was presented by the meeting on the 23rd February last, that the Company have been interested in collieries and steamboats throughout.

Mr. Powell: Will you state anything that you have in proof of what you assert?

The Chairman: I stated it possibly before you came into the room. There was a denial on the part of Mr. Jackson, that the West Hartlepool Company possessed directly or indirectly any coal property, or that they had any responsibility or connection with the working of any such property.

Mr. Baker.—That is only a denial on his part. Is there any proof on the other side?

The Chairman.—I am now going to inform you that this report of the committee—which nobody except the person who wrote the article could get a sight of before the meeting—was absolutely concealed from the meeting until after the chairman, Mr. Jackson, had taken the chair and opened the business of the meeting, when a man went round with the report of Mr. Sturge and the report of the directors in his hands, to distribute among those who were present.

Mr. Joseph Thompson.—I see the committee's report is dated the 20th of December.

The Chairman.—Yes it is; I suppose it would be sent to the directors at that time. Now I wish to draw your attention to this report of the committee. It does not at all bear out the foreshadowing of it which appeared on the 7th of December, in order to prepare the way and let the directors down easily; and it gave me the idea—it is a matter on which you are quite as capable of forming an opinion as I am—that between the time when this *Railway Times* article was penned and the presentation of the report, it has been materially altered still further "to make things pleasant" between the committee and the directors for an ulterior object, as I think I can shew in the Bill which is now before Parliament.

A Shareholder.—How many days intervened between the publication in the newspaper and the date of the report?

The Chairman—The date of the paper is the 17th of December, and the committee's report is dated "20th, 12th month." Now the report of the committee contains this paragraph—"The directors mainly in the infancy of the undertaking" (which is now 12 or 13 years old) "deemed it necessary to assist certain collieries on their lines of railway, in order to secure a large increase arising from the traffic of these collieries. Although this assistance has been large, yet the committee believe the collieries afford an adequate security for the payment of the interest, and ultimate payment of the principal of the money advanced." Now I wish to make a remark upon that. It appears now, in the face of that denial of Mr. Jackson, that mainly in the infancy of the undertaking, which would probably be from seven to ten years ago, assistance which is described as having been large, was rendered to those collieries of the chairman. I ask you, then, whether you consider that the denial that was given at the meeting of February, 1859, is as satisfactory as it ought to have been, and as it intended to be considered at the time?

Mr. Powell.—Will you read the denial again? I do not see the discrepancy myself.

The Chairman again read the paragraph in question.

Mr. Powell.—It appears to me to be perfectly consistent; the great inconsistency you were pointing out is no inconsistency at all.

Mr. Baker.—You have only to prove that the collieries in question are the collieries of Mr. Jackson; if you do that, I think you will fully carry out what you have stated.

Mr. Powell.—There is a denial of ownership in the one case, and a statement of a loan in the other; you say they are incompatible.

The Chairman.—I think you had better let me put it in my own way; I am as willing to be taught, and so receive information, as I am to teach and to give what I possess. If it all comes to nothing you will only have lost your time this morning, and it will be a very good thing for the Company, for you, as shareholders, for me, and for all of us.

Mr. Powell.—There are only two ways for us to adopt: the one for us to take notes of your speech as you proceed, and criticise it afterwards, and the other, when we hear any inconsistency to mention it at the moment.

The Chairman.—You have not yet allowed me to finish the proof I was about to offer of the inconsistency. The honorable proprietor says that "my original allegation was that the collieries belonged to the chairman, and that there is now only the proof of a loan." But this committee of assistance tells us that this state of things has been going on ever since the infancy of the undertaking, and that the assistance has been large." Now I want to know whether this has ever been entered in the Company's books? What information has ever been given to shareholders and to the landholders in the published accounts which are audited and found correct, of any dealing whatever between the Company and Mr. Jackson, or other owners, with respect either to collieries or steamboats? Is it to be borne that a gentleman is to be sole owner of some, and part owner of others, to the extent of ten collieries; that he is to be the chairman of an adjoining railway, and that he is to subsidise himself to any extent he pleases, or finds convenient? "The directors, mainly in the infancy of the undertaking, deemed it necessary to assist collieries on their lines of railway." Is that a thing that you, gentlemen, wish to be done with your money during a long series of years, without having any item in the accounts to give you the slightest information that one farthing has been given to support these collieries, or lines of steamboats to St. Petersburg, to Rotterdam, and to Hamburg? With regard to these steamboats, I am told the first thing done by the agents was to knock down the freight 50 per cent. They told shippers at Rotterdam, "We will take "goods between West Hartlepool and here at a reduction of 50 per cent." to start with; and, ultimately, they offered to take goods at at 2*s*. 6*d*. per ton less than anybody else would take them. Is that the way you, gentlemen, wish your money to be expended in fostering lines of steamers which you never hear of till they fail, and are foisted upon you?

Mr. Powell.—I must request you to be precise, and I must recal what you have said. You have shown to the meeting that there has been a denial of ownership of the collieries, and what you now allege is the proof of a loan. I am willing to accept that, but you have jumped to the conclusion for which you have given no premises; namely, that there has been a loan to collieries in which Mr. Jackson was interested. You have stated that broadly, without having given the least proof of it.

The Chairman.—I really think it was hardly worth while to interrupt for the purpose of saying that, for the real point of the question is, whether there has been a diversion of this Company's funds to support either Mr. Jackson's or any other collieries. It does not matter which.

Mr. Powell.—Confine it then to a general statement.

The Chairman.—I shall not confine it to a general statement.

Mr. Powell.—That point is admitted in the report.

The Chairman.—I am coming to the report; I know what is admitted, and I also know when it was admitted, and why it was admitted. I have shewn you the terms in which the charge was denied by Mr. Jackson.

Mr. Rowley.—I really must interrupt you, for my time is of some value to me; at present it does not appear to me that you have ever touched the question for which the meeting was convened; my desire is that you should come to the point for which the meeting is convened. I have sat here for an hour; I am interested in the concern.

THE CHAIRMAN.—If it is not worth your while to sit here and to sit quietly, it would be much better for you to leave if you have other more important business to attend to.

MR. ROWLEY.—It is worth my while.

THE CHAIRMAN.—I think it is indeed.

MR. ROWLEY.—But not to sit here and hear the desultory conversation which the gentleman occupying the chair at present has indulged in.

MR. THOMPSON.—I must say I feel very great interest in the observations which have been made by Mr. Wilkinson. Mr. Rowley had the advantage of attending the meeting held this day week; I have only had the advantage of reading an account of it in a penny paper which I have in my hand. Certainly these revelations to me are very interesting, and I should like to know the end of them.

A SHAREHOLDER.—So should I, exceedingly.

MR. POWELL.—I ask that we may not have these assertions, for which there is no proof even in outline. I have been asked broadly to accept as proved a statement given merely in the way that counsel would state generally his evidence—that there had been assistance given to collieries in which Mr. Jackson was concerned; that statement has been based upon the proof that assistance was given to some collieries. The one statement is general, the other is precise. I say there is no evidence to show that Mr. Jackson was concerned in the collieries to which assistance was given!

MR. COLEMAN.—With the permission of the chairman I will endeavour to put this point right. I think that point ought to be established, and perhaps Mr. Wilkinson did diverge a little from it: I hold in my hand the report of the last meeting, and Mr. Rowley, who took a conspicuous part in it and whom I am happy to see present, will be able to corroborate it. Now I pressed the chairman particularly with reference to the steamboats and collieries, and I asked him this question: "The object of my question is to know whether the Company possess any money interest in these steam vessels?" and the chairman said, "Certainly, they have done so for several years." I added, "And the collieries?" and the chairman said, "Yes." I then asked him, "Had they prior to this meeting?" the chairman replied, "Yes, certainly." I then said, "Has that ever been stated before in any of your reports?" and he said, "It was stated last year when you stood where you now are." Now no such statement was made. I had omitted to ask that particular question, and I was twitted afterwards for not having asked the question, because it would have been answered in the negative. Now here is an observation on the subject which I will read to you: "As regards the imputation on Mr. Jackson, after all the flourishings about his enormous collieries and steamboat transactions of the Company, not a syllable did Mr. Coleman breathe of either before the meeting." This is from the *Durham Advertiser*, one of the strongest supporters of Mr. Jackson, and which is written under his inspection. Here Mr. Jackson positively states that no colliery transactions and steamboat transactions had taken place; and in a letter to me 12 months ago, he denied that the Company owned any such property. Now the colliery transactions and steamboats are asserted to be the Company's transactions.

MR. BARRETT.—Does Mr. Sturge identify in any way the collieries which were assisted by the funds of the Company?

THE CHAIRMAN.—The committee are studiously silent upon that point, and I think that is a very pregnant circumstance. I think if we find that for many years, for a long series of years, beginning from "the infancy of the undertaking"—large assistance has been rendered to collieries, of which all they can now say is that they "afford an adequate security for the payment of the interest and ultimate repayment of the principal," we ought to know something more about them—we ought to know what coal mines they are: at present that information has not been given in print. I ask whether if any of you, gentlemen, had been in the position of the chairman of this Company, and you had known, what now appears to have been the state of the case, that for a long series of years you had been assisting collieries and steam boats, and that some rumour of this had got out, that the extent of the assistance was possibly some four or five hundred thousand pounds—I ask whether you would not think it was a little disingenuous to put out such a statement as that—"That the West Hartlepool Company do not possess, directly or indirectly, one inch of coal property in the kingdom, and that they have no responsibility connected with the working of any such property?" I ask, is that dealing fairly with the shareholders, and giving them that information as to the disposal of their money which they have a right to expect at the hands of the persons who are entrusted with the disposal of it? I look upon directors as the law does, simply as trustees for the benefit of shareholders, not of themselves; and when they are asked questions of this sort, I think the least we can expect is that they will afford us adequate information. I put it to you whether you are satisfied with the information and the candour of the statement which Mr. Jackson made upon that occasion?

Now I will pass on to the next point in the committee's report, by which it appears that "the Company are also interested in steam vessels,"—this is the first information given to us that we are interested in steam vessels—"which, though they may at first be advantageous to a company establishing a new seaport, yet, as they have not hitherto obtained special powers in respect of them,"—that is, the Company has no right to hold them now, nor ever to have had any dealings with them—"the committee recommend that, in the absence of such powers, such arrangements be made as shall free the company from any liability arising from being interested in ships or as carriers by sea." Here it seems that we have made rather a mistake. In the first instance we have made the mistake of laying out the company's funds in certain shipping speculations, which we had no business to entertain at all; and further, it appears that they are not very profitable speculations, and that we should now get rid of them as fast as we can. Now I want to know what means we had, if our money has been dealt with in this way, of forming an opinion upon the propriety or impropriety of these dealings with the steam boats and collieries? When was information ever given to us that probably half a million of our money has been laid out for these purposes? Were we ever consulted about it at all? Did we know till this moment that we had anything to do with collieries? Did we know till now, when they are to be paid for, that we had anything to do with steam boats? Where, in what secret books, have the returns and accounts been kept, and where has been the interest which we have received for those loans and disbursements? We have never had anything of the kind laid before us. And now I want you to mark this: as I told you before—this report of Mr. Sturge and the report of the directors were put into the hands of gentlemen at the meeting, after the chairman had begun the business; and they contained a revelation, given to us for the first time, that instead of the capital of the Company being unexhausted to the amount of £335,000, as it was stated to be at the meeting in February, 1859, "the Company's preferential and share capital and liabilities exceeded together, by about £500,000, the parliamentary power of the Company; but on a very cautious estimate of the value of the landed property, the *securities* in the collieries and the steam vessels, the committee are of opinion that their present value exceeds that amount, and that their prospective value is much greater. It is proposed by the Bill, which the committee will presently refer to, to increase the capital to that extent."—Namely, the extent of £500,000. Now if you are perfectly satisfied with that, I have nothing to say, but that I think you are a very trusting set of gentlemen, that you should be willing that half a million of your money should be expended on very little information being rendered to you, and much more being avowedly withheld from you; and further, that you should be willing that very few questions should be asked about it; for, with the exception of Mr. Coleman asking a few questions with respect to collieries, for the purpose of eliciting some information, there was not a word said by any persons present at the general meeting, except in laudation of the chairman; and I believe Mr. Rowley was so satisfied with the state of affairs, and the satisfactory manner in which the accounts had been kept, that he almost insisted on Mr. Coleman coming to the table and begging the chairman's pardon for making the charges against the accounts which he had done at the previous meeting. If it is so natural that so many people should be satisfied with the dealings of the chairman and directors, I can only say that I, for one, am not satisfied; and I tell you fairly at once that I have presented a petition to the House of Commons, and that I shall present one in due time to the House of Lords if it be necessary, to have a publication of these accounts, which has never been given us yet.

Mr. Powell.—I understand you to say that Mr. Sturge has given the matter a thorough investigation?

The Chairman.—I am assured that he has done so; but, unfortunately, he has not given us the result of it.

Mr. Powell.—Then you charge Mr. Sturge with concealment?

The Chairman.—It is not my business to bring a charge against anybody, but to bring before you printed documents; and if you are satisfied with these statements, I presume you wont ask for any further accounts.

Mr. Powell.—You have done more than bring documents—you make an inferential charge.

The Chairman.—You will see that it does not depend upon what I have said; I am only giving you something like a history.

Mr. Barrett.—It is perfectly true that the Act does not give power to invest in collieries or shipping; and there has been a clear case of *ultra vires* on the part of the directors to that extent. With regard to Mr. Jackson, or the other directors of the Company being owners of these collieries, it was a pity that it did not occur to Mr. Coleman to ask the question of the chairman at the meeting.

The Chairman.—The reason why he did not ask every question is, I believe, that at the meeting there might be 100 or 120 shareholders present, and out of them 119 were perfectly satisfied with these accounts. Mr. Coleman was the only person who was not satisfied, and I do not know that it is at all surprising that a gentleman who goes down from London to West Hartlepool, standing in such a position as that, should not like to stand up in the presence of 119 gentlemen, every one of whom was most bitterly opposed to him, and were apparently satisfied with the accounts. What I want is that we should arrive at a similar happy frame of mind ourselves. *I* want to be satisfied as to the accounts. If they are satisfied I am not, because I have not seen them. Indeed there is nothing in the accounts but what gives me the greatest distrust. This report of Mr. Sturge, and the report of the directors, are put into the hands of the persons present after the meeting has commenced. This meeting lasts two hours and forty minutes. The report of Mr. Sturge refers to a copy of the Bill which he says accompanies the report. There were no copies of the Bill given, but everything was taken in such a gregarious way by the meeting, as if they were a flock of sheep, that no observation whatever was made with reference to the Bill dealing with the affairs of the Company.

Mr. Rowley.—The bill was gone through clause by clause.

The Chairman.—The marginal notes only were read.

Mr. Coleman, to Mr. Rowley.—You know it was done as hurriedly as it was possible to do it. I declare that the Chairman said, 'It is not necessary to go through it clause by clause,' and the mere marginal notes were read.

Mr. Rowley.—That is going through it clause by clause.

The Chairman.—He did not read it clause by clause, but it was done in the utmost confusion.

Mr. Coleman.—In fact all the reporters, with one exception had left the room, thinking the meeting was over.

Mr. Rowley.—What had the reporters leaving the room to do with the matter? It was gone through clause by clause, and if Mr. Coleman did not attend to it, it was because he did not think proper to do so.

The Chairman.—I shall draw the attention of the meeting to the subject, and no doubt Mr. Rowley, as he so thoroughly understood the clauses of the Bill, will be able to enlighten us further on that most important subject.

Mr. Rowley.—I am come here to be enlightened,

The Chairman.—I hoped that you would enlighten me, because all my observations are tending to the point of the bill, which you know you say was so carefully explained to, and understood by the meeting.

Mr. Rowley.—That is the point I am upon.

The Chairman.—I suppose I am very dull, and am going a very roundabout way to work. but I cannot make myself afresh just on the spur of the moment. I must go through it my own way.

A SHAREHOLDER.—Is Mr. Rowley a director?

MR. ROWLEY.—No; I am only a shareholder. I am come here for information. If all these misdoings exist, there is no person in this room more interested in having them corrected than myself.*

MR. BARRETT.—Are you satisfied with the employment of the capital in collieries?

MR. ROWLEY.—If it is worth while to answer questions as we go on, I will do it with pleasure. I am only afraid of interrupting the chairman.

MR. BARRETT.—I thought you seemed satisfied with the conduct of the directors. It is an admitted fact, that the directors have advanced money to assist collieries, and it is clear from Mr. Sturge's report that they have invested the money of the Company in steamboats. Are you satisfied with that?

MR. ROWLEY.—I am perfectly satisfied with the report.

THE CHAIRMAN.—What I want to impress upon the meeting is this. Here is a discrepancy—to use no other term—acknowledged by Mr. Sturge, to the extent of £500,000, in addition to the £335,000 "unexhausted," which is made known for the first time to the shareholders during the meeting; and there is not a single question asked by any independent shareholder about it, so that we are entirely without information as to the way in which this great increment of the capital has been occasioned.

MR. ROWLEY.—You have not read the other part of Mr. Sturge's report. You certainly did read it, but you have not commented upon it.

THE CHAIRMAN.—You will be able to do that if I should not.

MR. ROWLEY.—I mean where he states that he has made the most searching and cautious estimate of the value of the landed property, and the securities in the collieries and steam vessels, and that he finds there is much more than sufficient to ensure the outlay.

MR. COLEMAN.—Does Mr. Sturge say that? Did not the *land* always belong to the Company?

MR. ROWLEY.—Unless my memory betrays me.

THE CHAIRMAN.—That is not the question.

MR. ROWLEY.—It is the whole question.

THE CHAIRMAN.—It may be with you, but not with me. I want to know what has become of all the money, and in what way it has been expended.

MR. ROWLEY.—The committee on the one hand state that the directors have exhausted their powers, and on the other hand they say that they have made a cautious estimate of the value of the property, and that it exceeds the outlay.

MR. THOMPSON.—I think we ought to allow Mr. Wilkinson to complete his statement.

THE CHAIRMAN.—If I have found a mare's nest, it will be of great advantage to the Company and to you that it should all be fairly explained.

MR. ROWLEY.—I think we had better not interrupt the chairman.

THE CHAIRMAN.—I think so too. I have stated that during the two hours and forty minutes which the meeting lasted, no question was asked, and no statement was made of the manner in which the capital and the Parliamentary powers have been exceeded. I think it is very necessary and desirable that we should know something about it.

MR. ROWLEY.—If you would read the second clause it would convey a great deal of information.

THE CHAIRMAN.—I have read it.

MR. ROWLEY.—You did read it, but the gentlemen did not understand it.

THE CHAIRMAN.—Then I will read it again. "The Company's preferential share capital and liabilities exceed together by £500,000 the Parliamentary powers of the Company, but in a very cautious estimate of the value of the landed property, the securities in the collieries and the steam vessels, the Committee are of opinion that their present value exceeds that amount, and that

---

* Mr. Rowley was a most decided partizan; he said to a shareholder present, "That man Coleman is mad." The gentleman, who happened to know me in private life, replied, "There is a good deal of method in his madness."

their prospective value is much greater. It is proposed by the Bill, which the Committee will presently refer to, to increase the capital to that extent." If Mr. Rowley thinks I did not make any observations upon that, I will make some now. And in the first place I shall draw your attention to this fact, " that the Committee found that the parliamentary capital has been exceeded by £500,000." Now, you must bear in mind that at the meeting in February, 1859, the parliamentary capital was stated to be unexhausted to the extent of £335,000. Therefore I wish you to remember that this £500,000 clearly represents £835,000 which the Committee of investigation have discovered to have been concealed from the knowledge of the shareholders, until the moment when this report is placed in their hands. I do not know whether that makes the matter more clear to Mr. Rowley, but to me it is perfectly clear that here is a deficiency, arising in some way, of £835,000, in respect of which we have no information whatever as to by whom it was expended, upon whom it was expended, upon whose authority it was expended, whose collieries these are that required this large assistance; whose steam boats these are which are now foisted on the Company; what has become of the accounts of this vast sum of money? During all the years that it has been out of the Company's pockets, what has become of the books in which the concealed transactions have been entered. Now, if we have been wasting anything like £835,000 ——

Mr. Rowley.—It is not asserted.

The Chairman.—I want to know then where it is gone.

Mr. Rowley.—You say the Committee have found that £800,000 has been advanced. It is not so.

The Chairman.—I say the Committee said " that the Company's preferential and share capital and liabilities exceed together by £500,000 the parliamentary powers of the Company."

Mr. Rowley.—That is not £800,000.

The Chairman.—I say, in addition, that in February, 1859, at the previous meeting to this, the directors said " that the parliamentary powers of capital were unexhausted to the extent of £335,000." Adding the two sums together you get £835,000; as to which there is not one syllable of information given to us. Indeed, in the way it is asked at our hands by the reports and the Bill in parliament, it can only be considered as " secret service" money to be at the disposal of the directors.

Mr. Rowley.—That is a total misapprehension.

The Chairman.—Then I wish you would make it comprehensible. If you will address yourself particularly to that point it will be greatly for the information of myself, and perhaps of some other gentlemen. Why is all this left to inference? Surely the figures are large enough to make it desirable that the directors should have stated them, or should state them now.

Mr. Baker.—I think the chairman has put it very fairly, and that no answer has been given to it.

The Chairman.—I know some gentlemen may be weary; and I may not state it sufficiently curtly. I will now proceed, at the risk of omitting some circumstances, to the bill itself. Now, it is said lawyers are very bad accountants, and I may have made another mistake about this, but it would appear to me that if the Parliamentary powers of the Company were £2,686,000, and it had been discovered that they had exceeded by half a million, it would have been quite enough to have taken powers to raise that half million, and that would have brought us to £3,186,000; but instead of that, the sum proposed to be raised by the clause which I shall have to bring before you is, £3,300,000. I own that the secret and round way in which figures are dealt with in this Company, it is not a very astounding thing to me that upwards of £120,000 should be just put down for odd money, and that I should find in clause 21 of the bill that there are additional powers given to raise the sum to £500,000 to be in addition to the rights of the present debenture holders. Now, I should tell you that it has been roundly stated, and was stated at the last meeting, to Mr. Jackson's face, that there has been an over issue of debentures altogether unauthorised by the Company. Now, whether any of you hold debentures of that sort or not, I am sure I cannot tell. I believe the debentures are issued under the common seal of the Company, without any signature being attached to them, but how that may be I cannot tell. But it is a very awkward position for us to be in, to have it broadly stated to the chairman's face that there has been an over issue of debentures.

A Shareholder.—Not properly signed, I understand.

The Chairman.—Irregularly issued was the charge.

Mr. Rowley.—Who is that stated by?

Mr. Coleman.—By me. I dared the chairman to put me to the proof of the assertion, and what did the chairman say to it? He said, "I do not dare you to do anything." I stated this to the chairman in the face of Mr. Rowley, and all his other supporters, "I tell you, sir, since you put it to me, that I accuse you of issuing irregular bonds, and when they were questioned on the market you hastily withdrew them by sending your cheque for the amount, and I dare you and your supporters to put me to the proof of it." The chairman replied, "I do not dare you to do anything."

Mr. Rowley.—He did not wish to be troubled with it.

The Chairman.—I am quite sure that the Chairman *did not* wish to be troubled with it.

Mr. Baker.—Were the irregular bonds withdrawn?

Mr. Coleman.—We will discuss that, if you please, afterwards; I shall be glad to give you any information on the subject.

The Chairman.—I now refer to the ninth page of the Bill, part of the preamble, where, at the thirtieth line, you have this recital, "And whereas the aggregate amount which the Company have laid out, or are in the course of expending, or must necessarily expend upon the undertaking, will amount to the sum of £3,400,000, subject only to reduction when certain property of the Company of the estimated value of upwards of £500,000 becomes available for that purpose." Here, then, is a recital that the Company have laid out, or are in the course of expending, or must necessarily expend upon the undertaking, a sum of £3,400,000; there is no divisions of these sums, as I should have thought it would have been proper to make.

Mr. Rowley.—There is in former clauses.

The Chairman.—No, I beg your pardon. I should like to know what is the amount laid out, what is the amount in the course of expending, and the estimate of what must necessarily be expended, and for what purpose to be approved by us such expenditure is to be made. But there is no information whatever given to us as to explain that, and as to why the capital is suddenly increased to this sum, which, including the £335,000 unexhausted in February, 1859, makes the increase 1,048,857 1*s.* 8*d.*; and there is a power given by clause 21, to borrow £500,000 in addition. The two summaries of balance sheets for 1858 and 1859, shew an unexplained and sudden discrepancy of nearly £550,000 between them, the increase being principally in the first two items of the account in 1859. It was said at the meeting by Mr. R. W. Jackson, the chairman, that the discrepancy between the Company's accounts and those returned to the Board of Trade, arose from there not being sufficient columns in the Board of Trade returns to comprise the items. That I have ascertained at the Board of Trade not to be the case. Now I turn to the next page of the Bill, where it speaks of the before-mentioned aggregate sum of £3,400,000, representing "the preferential capital, the ordinary consolidated stock, money advanced in respect of preference and ordinary consolidated stock, credited by the Company, money raised on mortgage or bond, and ALL THE LIABILITIES of the Company in respect of additional rolling stock and works in progress, or which they must necessarily provide or complete." I want to ask the gentlemen who are so accurately acquainted and so perfectly satisfied with the wording of this Bill, what is the meaning of the words "money advanced in respect of preference and ordinary consolidated stock?" The ordinary acceptation of it, as I should read it, would be that the directors or that somebody has been borrowing money on deposit —money advanced in respect of preference and ordinary consolidated stock. I want to know what that means, and what the amount of liabilities are under that head. Having established the position that there are some very large liabilities of the Company that are unprovided for, because there is over issue to the extent of £835,000 to be provided for, I come to the matter which more immediately presses upon the bondholders; and I refer to page 13 of the Bill, where you have the interpretation clause of the Act, which is ordinarily passed over as not of any very great consequence. It generally escapes attention, but there is at the twentieth line this remarkable expression; it is a definition of what the words "debenture holders" are to mean, in dealing with them under this Act:—"The expression 'debenture holders' means the holders of mortgages and bonds, and *other creditors* of the Company, at the time of the passing of this Act." Now I am a debenture holder, and there is nothing in this Act to tell me that the whole of that deficiency of £835,000 is not represented by "other creditors." Now I may have £835,000 of "other creditors" billeted upon me, and they are to have equal priority with me, and we are all to come in after the preference stocks have been satisfied. Now it may possibly be very proper that they should so come, but I should like to know who they are; I should like to know what business simple contract creditors of the Company have to come and rank equally with me as a debenture holder. Is that the way we are to have foisted upon us something like a million of money under the loose designation, "other creditors of the Company?"

Mr. Rowley.—Does not clause 8 answer your question?

The Chairman.—We will come to that presently. You must remember that no words are ever put into an Act of Parliament without intending to have some meaning attached to them. I want to know what meaning is attached to them in this case.

Mr. Rowley.—Had you not better answer your own question? I think clause 8 answers it.

The Chairman.—Clause 8 is this:—"The arrangement as regards the shareholders shall take effect when the shareholders have assented thereto as in this Act provided; and as regards the debenture holders, with respect to those holders as assent thereto, but the arrangement shall not be dependant upon the assent of all the debenture holders: provided always that the rights of the debenture holders who do not assent shall not be prejudiced or altered by the arrangement but shall continue as if the arrangement had not been made." Now that does not tell me anything of the decree whatever, because it says, "as regards the debenture holders, with respect to such of those holders who assent thereto, but the arrangement shall not be dependant upon the assent of all of them."

Mr. Rowley.—Those who do not assent shall not be affected by it.

The Chairman.—Look at the interpretation clause, which tells us what the term "debenture holders" means. It means debenture holders and *other creditors*. Therefore, other creditors will be allowed to come in as debenture holders; we shall have no difficulty in obtaining their assent.

Mr. Rowley.—The debenture holders are mentioned in clause 8, evidently alluding to the existing debenture holders.

The Chairman.—I do not think it is at all evidently.

Mr. Rowley.—It is stated in the clause immediately above No. 7, "The consent of the debenture holders shall be signified by writing under their hands."

The Chairman.—The term "debenture holders," as read by the interpretation clause, means debenture holders and other creditors.

Mr. Rowley.—It means existing debenture holders.

The Chairman.—Then it should say so.

Mr. Barrett.—I think that it must mean the debenture holders of the present time. It cannot apply to those who are going to be created.

Mr. Rowley.—It is as plain as daylight; and it is idle to discuss it.

Mr. Coleman.—Are you authorised by Mr. Bell, or Mr. Jackson, to say that?

Mr. Rowley.—No.

The Chairman.—Are they here to answer these questions; or were they at the last meeting to answer them?

Mr. Rowley.—I am here to answer for myself.

Mr. Coleman.—If Mr. Bell or Mr. Sturge were here it would be a different thing; but you say you are not authorised to state what you have told us, and therefore it is of no value.

Mr. Rowley.—I am only commenting upon the bill.

The Chairman.—Where is Mr. Bell?—Where is Mr. Sturge?

Mr. Rowley.—I have nothing to do with them.

Mr. Coleman.—Yes, you have.

Mr. Rowley.—I am not in the habit of making mis-statements; and I will thank you not to contradict me upon a question that I am capable of answering for myself.

Mr. Coleman.—I do not wish to get into conflict with you; but I hope to satisfy your mind that you have been in a grievous error. You have done me grievous injustice; and you cannot be surprised at the state of my feelings, with your remarks at the late meeting ringing in my ears.

The Chairman.—I ought to mention, as a very important thing indeed, that neither Mr. Sturge nor Mr. Bell was present at the meeting at Hartlepool, to give any information whatever.

Mr. Rowley. Will you give us this information on the Act of Parliament—I am much interested in it.

The Chairman.—I will not be put off from stating, and that in the most prominent way, that Mr. Sturge, and Mr. Bell, and Mr. Hudson, the accountant who at the previous meeting had certified the accounts of the Company to be correct, were most conveniently absent at this meeting; and I take it, an obvious inference is, that they were absent for good reasons of their own; that they knew too much of the state of these accounts; and that there would have been a revelation had they been present, which it would have been impossible to avoid. Now look at clause 28.

Mr. Rowley.—Really this is very important. I am a large bondholder, and I want to know whether I am as insecure as you describe.

Mr. Coleman.—Ask your friend, Mr. Jackson—or Mr. Bell!

The Chairman.—You wont take my opinion; you had better go to your own solicitor, and take counsel's opinion upon it. The 28th clause is a very remarkable one: "Subject to the provisions of this Act, and so as not to prejudice or affect any priority between the debenture holders" (who are by the interpretation clause made to consist of debenture holders and other creditors) "or the rights of the debenture holders, the several mortgages and bonds issued by the Company before the passing of this Act, for such part of the sum of £3,400,000 as is represented by the paid-up preferential and ordinary consolidated shares and stock in the Company shall *without respect to the original issue thereof* be deemed to be mortgages and bonds issued under the authority of this Act for securing an equivalent sum, part of the aggregate amount which the Company are by this Act authorized to borrow." Now, I say distinctly, in the absence of the accounts which ought to have been presented to the meeting, that these words distinctly point as much as I can do now with my finger to some over issue, some defalcation with respect to these bonds, "shall without respect to the original issue thereof be deemed mortgages and bonds." Here it brings in all the other creditors of the Company clearly upon us. The other most important matter as to which I wish to ascertain whether those who are really interested in this railway are aware of it or not, is with respect to the division of this Company into two. The Act of Parliament that I have been reading provides for the division of this undertaking into two. The Act of 1852, was for the purpose of uniting the docks and the railway; this Bill is for the purpose of disuniting them and of asking the shareholders to contribute their bond and share capital, in certain proportions, between the docks and the railway. I ask with all this luminous information which has been furnished to us by the directors and by Mr. Sturge in what proportions you think proper to allocate your claims against this Company to the two. There is to be, as soon as this Bill passes, a division, and that is put forward as the main-spring of this whole application to Parliament—it is for the purpose of dividing this into two undertakings and having separate accounts kept—providing that the Railway Company shall have a capital of two millions, and that the docks and harbour shall represent a capital of £1,400,000, and you are asked, as soon as the Bill is passed, in what proportions you will take either to the one or the other. I ask you what information has been given to you to enable you to make this division? Has any estimate been made? If it has been, has it been furnished to us showing us in the first place why there should be any such division at all, and in the next place in what proportions we ought to be asked to allocate our capital? I think these are matters very important for us to know. It seems to me a remarkable thing that we should have this Act of Parliament bringing in an unexplained amount of creditors and other liabilities to rank equally with us as bondholders; and then, that they and we are to be asked to allocate our capital to either one or the other of these two undertakings.

For my own part, it has always been considered that the main advantage in the whole concern was that the railway and the docks were connected and mutually assisting one another; but now the two are to be divided, and we are to divide our capital between the two. I say, there has been no reason given for that except the statement, that it is possible that the Government will establish a harbour of refuge, and that if it does, it may be expedient for the Company to make over the docks and harbour to a public body. I, for one, do not very much approve of the two things being disunited. If there is any value in the connection, I wish to keep it; and I do not wish to hand over half of my capital, or any portion of it, to be dealt with, for the public interest, by a public body in that way. I confess I am not satisfied with the reasons that are given; I am not satisfied with the accounts that have been rendered to us. There is a total absence of information to explain this discrepancy of £835,000. If it was right to apply that or any portion of that sum to collieries and steam boats during a long course of years, I think in common fairness and honesty those shareholders who have trusted their money to the directors should have been consulted; and that if they had not originally been consulted, from some cause hitherto unexplained, it would have been proper at all events that we should have been credited with the interest of this money. But the whole thing from beginning to end, as far as information is given to us to satisfy us as to this deficiency or defalcation, is comprised in the two paragraphs which I have read from Mr. Sturge's report, as to the directors having assisted collieries, and as to the Company being also interested in some steam vessels. There are other statements made in the directors' report, but I feel that I have occupied your time at such a length that I ought not to refer to them. If you are satisfied, I am not satisfied. I am in a position fortunately to appeal to the House of Commons for the accounts, and for such information as they may think I am entitled to. If it had not been for a very remarkable circumstance, it would have been impossible that I should have been in that position. By a curious coincidence, if there are any coincidences, the time for petitioning against this bill expired on the afternoon of the day on which this meeting was held at West Hartlepool. At the time when the meeting is held at which this revelation is made—on that very day the time expires for petitioning against the bill. I think there is a disingenuousness and a reticence in furnishing information with respect to these matters, which we have a perfect right to feel aggrieved at. I do feel aggrieved at it, and if you do not, I am satisfied, and I shall proceed to do what I have stated, altogether irrespective of you; if you are dissatisfied, and like to give me your moral support, I shall be very grateful for it. If you do not, you have a perfect right to be satisfied with the investment of your money; and I wish you pleasant dreams, and hope it may never trouble you at nights. With regard to the division of the capital, the railway is to represent £2,000,000, and the docks are to represent the balance of £1,400,000, with borrowing powers to each in addition.

Mr. Baker.—The railway without the harbour is almost valueless.

The Chairman.—It appears to me to be so, but really we are all in the dark. There may be a perfectly good answer to be given to all this, but what I say is, it has not been given yet, and I shall be very glad if I can get it.

Mr. Coleman.—I do not know whether Mr. Rowley is going to offer any observations, if he is, I shall be happy to make way.

Mr. Rowley.—No; I have nothing to say.

Mr. Coleman.—I am very glad above all others to see Mr. Rowley here whom I had the disagreeable necessity of opposing, or rather he opposed me, at the West Hartlepool meeting last week. Mr. Rowley on that occasion made some very strong observations. I am not now going into any personal question, but I wish to bring Mr. Rowley's attention to these matters, not to create an ill-feeling on his part, or on the part of any one.

Mr. Powell.—May I be allowed to say, and I say it without the slightest discourtesy, that we have been here for two hours and ten minutes, and I trust, therefore, that your observations will be very short.

Mr. Coleman.—My observations are very important to myself, but, perhaps, not to you. I stand in a peculiar position here. I have had a great deal of obloquy thrown upon me for the part I have taken in this affair. I cannot hope for an opportunity of saying all I desire at West Hartlepool where the meetings are held only once a year, where the chairman has 99 out of a hundred sympathising with his views, where he comes prepared with a number of cut-and-dried resolutions of the most complimentary kind, and where he is always so fortunate as to have a gentleman of the standing of Mr. Rowley to throw his mantle over him.*

Mr. Rowley.—I have only been once in my life.

Mr. Coleman.—I say, some one or another similar to yourself. And on this last occasion you were certainly his great shield and helpmate.

Mr. Rowley.—I wished to be so.

Mr. Colemn.—Well, you succeeded in that partisan-packed assembly. My opportunities are very few. I do not want to enter into the personal question as between Mr. Jackson and myself, for that is a question with which of course this meeting has nothing to do. But if any gentleman wishes to know the real facts of the case, I shall be most happy to state them to him at any time privately, and I am not afraid of any disadvantage to myself by such investigation. Now, as to the contradictions which we allege to exist in Mr. Jackson's statements, I was surprised to find that the steamboats and collieries were about to be imposed upon this Company, and when I asked a question respecting it the chairman said, point blank, that they had always belonged to the Company. It was one of the charges I originally made against the chairman that he had been using, as Mr. Wilkinson has stated, the funds of the Company for the purpose of fostering these things, and it had been as stoutly denied. The contradiction arises from the letter which has been read, a portion of a letter which he addressed to me last year, in which he disclaims these things, as having nothing to do with the Company.

Mr. Powell.—I profess to understand English, but you confound your ideas with Mr. Jackson's words.

Mr. Coleman.—I know there is a great peculiarity in Mr. Jackson's words; but there is no mistake about this, that he said they have not one inch of colliery property in the kingdom attached to the Company.

The Chairman.—It would have been much better for them if they had—if they have been giving this assistance so many years to a large extent.

Mr. Coleman.—Allow me to give you the real reading of this case. Mr. Sturge came to me under the circumstances described. I placed the fullest confidence in him—he was, I thought, fully entitled to it; and he undertook, as you have been told, to investigate this matter thoroughly. He desired above all things that I should be silent in the matter until he was master of the position. Mr. Rowley at the meeting accused me of having twelve months to think over these statements, and had failed to prove anything; but, I suppose, he was not aware that I had never been asked a question on this point by Mr. Sturge himself. Mr. Sturge seemed to be satisfied from the very outset that there was something manifestly wrong, for he said, "You will be justified; that is all I can say at present." What could I wish more than that I should be justified? How could I be justified if all was right? I accordingly held my peace, and suffered all the disadvantage and the obloquy thrown upon me by the papers supporting Mr. Jackson's views. I suffered much disadvantage in consequence of my silence; and I went to the last meeting, hoping to find that his report was to be in substance what Mr. Sturge had promised it should be. But, what was my surprise to find it stated in this paragraph, which Mr. Wilkinson has not read to you: "Mr. Benjamin Coleman, at the general meeting of the Company held on the 25th February, 1859, having disavowed being actuated by any improper motive for the course which he took in drawing the attention of the shareholders to the state of the Company's affairs, the committee consider that the shareholders are indebted to him for having called their particular attention to the position of the Company, with a view to its improvement." That is to say, that having condoned some errors, the committee forgave me,

* I have reason to believe that the last meeting was composed of men, many of whom are not shareholders, and most of them having a direct interest in supporting Mr. Jackson at any cost.

and, therefore, they thanked me for having called their attention to the subject. Why *should* they thank me? I did a great deal more than disavow being actuated by improper motives.—I impugned the correctness of the Company's accounts; and I said at the last meeting, "I am here to maintain my position." And I said further, that the chairman had tampered with the bonds; and I told him so to his face—I dared him to put me to to the proof of it. Did Mr. Jackson rise with indignation from his seat and repudiate the charge I made against him? No, he sat perfectly still; and what did he say? "I do not dare you to do anything." And what did he say afterwards? He almost asked me to shake hands with him, wishing to God that I might forget this matter, and not persecute him, which term I repudiated, and he withdrew. I am now pursuing this as a matter of character. It is not a question as to the amount I hold; and I defy Mr. Rowley, or any other gentleman who supports Mr. Jackson, to point out a single act of mine that disentitles me to their fullest confidence. I have acted throughout in the most open manner, and have done nothing in an underhand way. I now deliberately charge the chairman and the directors with having paid dividends out of capital to a very considerable extent, and in particular some £11,000 or £12,000, in April, 1858, to which I called their attention last year. I say, that Mr. Jackson and others, whose names I have here, and will give them to you if you wish it, being partners in these steam boats and collieries, have from time to time used the bonds of the Company and the acceptances of the Company for the purpose of sustaining their private speculations. When Mr. Sturge stepped in and found the real state of the case, that Mr. Jackson has over-shot the mark by 5, or 6, or 7, or £800,000, whatever the amount may be, what does Mr. Sturge do? He does not tell you that he has found Mr. Jackson has conducted his accounts honourably, which Mr. Rowley has been so constantly harping upon; he says nothing of the kind; he is silent upon the whole of my charges. He keeps away from the meeting at West Hartlepool; and Mr. Bell, the only other man who could give information, kept away too; and when I appealed to Mr. Sturge, which I have done in a letter since my return, which is too long to be read, but which I shall publish—I say, when I appeal to him to know his reasons, he tells me, in effect, that he does not choose to give them. I am not going to read that letter, but I will read you a short letter which Mr. Sturge wrote to me, and that will not occupy two minutes. (*see* Correspondence.) I was going to give you my explanation of how the matter stands. Mr. Sturge finding that there was a "pretty kettle of fish," to use a common but expressive phrase, in this West Hartlepool concern, sought about for the best means by which he could make it right; and he delayed his reports for months to see, whilst he was breeding the bane, how he could find the antidote: and how does he find it? In these private steamers and these collieries, which you are to be forced to take, because you can get nothing else from Mr. Jackson—you are to be forced to take these collieries and steamers to make good the liabilities to which the Company have been committed, whether in bonds, or acceptances, or anything else. Now, sir, I believe this to be the true explanation; and if you reject that bill, you reject Mr. Jackson's acceptances, and let him pay them himself. He wants you to take his steamers, which have been loosing 10 or £20,000 a year, and which he has had the shamelessness now to say, had always belonged to this Company. I say, they belonged to him privately. I have the names of the parties here; and he used your credit for their purchase and support.

Mr. Rowley.—He denied that.

Mr. Coleman.—I know he denied it; but I can show you the custom house returns if you like. Here it is, the vessels are registered in several names, the chairman having the largest share. I repeat that this Bill is made simply for this purpose. Mr. Jackson having got into difficulties, makes over the best securities he can find to make good these deficiencies. Now listen to that Mr. Rowley. He is endeavouring to make good these deficiencies by his collieries and steam boats, and this Bill is a bill of indemnity. I say we are not bound to accept Mr. Jackson's liabilities and acceptances to the extent of tens of thousands of pounds in this or any other mode which this Bill is sought to cover.

Mr. Rowley.—You seem to be talking about proof, and treat things as if proved already.

MR. COLEMAN.—It ought not to be left for me to prove. The whole explanation ought to be volunteered by the directors, the committee, or Mr. Bell.

MR. ROWLEY.—But after all these false issues and things of that description, why didn't you prove them?

MR. COLEMAN.—Because, as I have already told you, they never asked me.

MR. ROWLEY.—You have all the disposition to do it, that is quite evident.

MR. COLEMAN.—I tell you I gave the information into the hands of Mr. Sturge, and he pledged his word to probe it to the bottom. I felt I could not leave it in better hands as far as sagacity went. He told me to be quiet; and that was his condition; therefore, I could not state these things till the present time. It was very unfair in Mr. Sturge, to turn round upon me at the last moment. I do not know whether you are acquainted with the subject of biology or not. I am; and I believe Mr. Jackson has a peculiarly strong power of this kind, a mesmeric power, so that every man who comes within the circle of his influence is biologised, and so brought to believe as he wishes, and that is something that really does not exist.

A VOICE.—All except yourself.

MR. COLEMAN.—Except myself. There are some persons you know who can withstand the influence, and you may fairly make that exception in my favor.

MR. BARRETT.—I thought the intention in calling this meeting was to consider whether you could make out a *prima facie* case against the Company in regard to the Bills now before Parliament. I do not know that we have anything to do with private disputes between Mr. Coleman and Mr. Jackson, and it is not for us to enter upon them. We are interested as debenture holders, or as preference shareholders, or in some other way in the Company. I agree with you that there are startling suggestions raised, and acts on the part of the directors that call from us for some expression of want of confidence in them as holding possession of our property. I must say, for one, that you have made a strong *prima facie* case, and one that ought to be further enquired into. As a debenture holder, I shall certainly support you, as far I possibly can, in your petition to Parliament in opposition to the present Bill. I think particularly that the 5th clause, where the debenture holders are to elect whether they will take the security which they hold from one property or from the other, is extremely objectionable. I also concur entirely with you in the observation which you have made in the 28th clause: I think the words there are very extraordinary, and I cannot make out what they can refer to, unless there has been something which has been very irregular in the proceedings of this Company. "And shall, without respect to the original issue thereof, be deemed to be mortgages and bonds issued by the Company." I say those are words that create a good deal of suspicion, and must call for observation.

MR. TAYLOR.—I wish to speak a word on this subject as a bondholder. I am aware that in the particular clause referred to, it does not mention whether the debenture stock is included in the £3,400,000; but in the previous clause, in dividing the property of the Company, it speaks of the amount as including the powers to borrow. To make myself sure upon the subject, I went yesterday to Mr. Bell, of the firm of Bell, Stewart, & Lloyd, and asked the question personally, and he told me that his opinion was, that the £3,400,000 included the debenture stock. He also said, "that I may be perfectly sure, I will ask Mr. Stewart, who drew the Bill, and if it is not so, I will write to you." I asked him to write to me whether or no, and I have his letter this morning, stating that the £3,400,000 includes the borrowing powers. I am speaking simply as a bondholder, and as interested for other bondholders. With regard to the statements that have been made, I am not here for a moment to say that there have not been irregular proceedings with regard to the assistance which has been given to the collieries, which is admitted by Mr. Sturge's committee. The question is now, what is the best position that we, as bondholders, can be placed in, admitting the circumstances as they are. Mr. Wilkinson has spoken about other creditors who are to rank as bondholders, but I do not take that as a proof that the debentures have been issued beyond the Parliamentary capital. There may be other creditors, but these extra creditors are not creditors as debenture holders. I merely give that as my opinion. With regard to the number of those creditors who are to rank with us as debenture holders, the power to borrow, the proportion of this £3,400,000 will be fixed by Act of Parliament according to the common regulations of the Board of Trade, which only allow a certain proportion of railway capital to be called up in the way of debentures. Now the increase of capital which this Bill proposes to give, is, in round numbers, £800,000. It does not appear that it will be required at once, because it speaks of progressive and future works of the Company; any one who knows anything of the district, knows that since the discovery of ironstone in the Cleveland district, the whole district is in a position of progress, and that in all the railways in the neighbourhood there will be a constant increase of capital. We are not to assume then, that this £3,400,000 is wanted for present purposes. The utmost which they can add to the debenture stock is £300,000, and the interest of that at £5 per cent. is £15,000. By the net revenue of the Company for 1859, after deducting £38,000 for debenture interest, there is a balance of £67,000, and we shall find, supposing that we, as bondholders, have held our bonds from 1857, are in the same position in 1860, as we were then. I am assuming that the bondholders have held their bonds from that time; at any rate, I hold that without putting any value upon the securities of the collieries which have been added to the property of the Company, and the steamboats taking them as *nil*, and taking no account of the 200 acres of land which the Company still holds, the revenues of the Company offer an ample margin of security to the bondholders; and admitting the irregularities which the committee speak of with regard to the assistance which has been given to these collieries, and in speaking of them, I cannot admit the Chairman's and Mr. Coleman's position, that these collieries and steamboats are to be viewed as a private speculation of Mr. Jackson. I believe that Mr. Jackson is not solely personally involved in these matters, and the committee give it as their opinion, and those who are most interested in the matter give it as their opinion, that the arrangement entered into with the collieries and steamboats, has been for the advantage of the Company. You see it in the merchandise and the traffic; I have known the district intimately for some years, and know the position of affairs.

The Chairman.—Here is a list of the collieries with the owners' names attached.

Mr. Taylor.—You know it does not prove the actual ownership.

Mr. Coleman.—This, of the steamboats, is from the custom house.

Mr. Taylor.—With reference to these steamboats, allow me to say that the merchandize traffic has risen, during the last six years, from a mere nothing to £52,000. Now, if there has been a loss upon the steamboats, the Company have gained an immense advantage in the merchandize, and have made West Hartlepool one of the first ports upon the east coast. Now, as a bondholder personally interested, and interested to a large extent as regards my clients, I say most emphatically that it is the interest of the bondholders to promote the speedy passing of this Bill, and that if we allow any feeling against Mr. Jackson, on any other person, to put us in the position of opponents of this Bill, we are acting most suicidally to our own interests, and acting very much like the man represented in the picture as sitting on a public house sign, and sawing it away, without thinking that he will come down with the crash. Therefore, with the greatest respect to Mr. Wilkinson, who is a personal friend of mine, I must say very decidedly that I object most entirely to his views. As interested personally to a larger extent than he is, and to a far greater extent as representing other people, I must say that our interests are to promote the speedy passing of this Bill.

Mr. Baker.—Though I believe Mr. Jackson may have done everything for the interests of the Company, I cannot support this Bill.

Mr. Coleman.—With regard to what Mr. Taylor has said, why should we not have the facts before us? Why should not Mr. Bell attend this meeting, as he was invited to do? Why did he not attend the general meeting of the Company, which he attended last year, when no Bill was proposed, to give the necessary information? Then, no difficulty would have arisen. I repeat, again, these collieries and steamboats are private speculations. With regard to the steamboats, I am informed that they lose from £10,000 to £20,000 a year. Now, are you going to take them and work them without knowing what you are going to do? That is really what you are asked to do, not by the Bill, but in a roundabout way. The chairman says they are already yours, but nobody else says they are; the Bill does not say so, and this committee's report does not say so. Mr. Rowley, who is now reading it, will see that they are taken as *securities*. How can he reconcile the statement of the chairman that they have been the company's property for years, with the fact there staring him in the face, *that they have been taken as securities?* What I want to warn you against, is this, £10,000 or £20,000 a year is lost by somebody, in the steamboat speculation. I know nothing of the merits of the collieries. I believe they do not pay, and if they do pay, it would be a fractional matter. The argument of Mr. Taylor is worth nothing to you as share and debenture holders, because he is arguing that you should take Mr. Jackson's liabilities, created in a manner that he has not explained. If, for instance, there are a hundred creditors holding a £1,000 acceptance each of this Company, are you prepared to say that you are going to allow this Bill to pass, and bring them in to you as bondholders? That is the case of this Bill. I do not know to what extent because they do not give us any explanation. Finding they cannot get anything else, they want to force this upon you as security, as the best you can get. If this is true, and nobody says it is not, the charges we have made are well founded. I may have but an insignificant sum in the concern, but that does not lesson the value of my statements.

Mr. Baker.—There is one question I wish to ask. Do the preference shareholders take precedence of the mortgagees?

Mr. Coleman.—Mr. Wilkinson thinks they do.

The Chairman.—I am sure they do, if I can read an Act of Parliament. I refer to the 96th section of the Act of 1852, in which it goes through these preference shares, A, B, C, and D, and says that they are to have priority over all mortgages bonds, debts, and charges affecting the Company.

Mr. Rowley said he was a considerable bondholder and shareholder in the Company, and was therefore greatly interested in its affairs. So far as his knowledge went, he concurred in the propriety of supporting the directors and committee of assistance. The objections they had heard had emanated from a gentleman interested to the extent of about £4,000; and he certainly thought if that gentleman had not been desirous of taking a course injurious to the Company, he might have easily transferred his bonds (which were held in good repute) to some one else. He (Mr. Rowley) regarded Mr. Coleman's statements with extreme distrust, and he had evidently come into the concern with the view of making a disturbance.

Mr. Coleman said he had been stopped for entering into personal matters, and that Mr. Rowley had no right to open the question.

The Chairman said that personal matters should not be introduced. He had opened the question himself as one resting entirely on facts. They had nothing to do with the disputes of Mr. Coleman and Mr. Jackson; the simple question being whether, as bondholders or shareholders, they were satisfied with the accounts and with the Bill before Parliament. Mr. Coleman might be a person of very bad character or of very good character. He (the chairman) believed him to be of very good character. He had personally investigated his statements, and had come to the conclusion that they were founded in fact. The meeting, however, should confine itself to the Bill and to the other matters in hand.

Mr. Rowley said that was his desire. He repeated that he had a considerable stake in the Company, and if he was not satisfied with the statements of the committee of assistance, he should be as anxious as Mr. Coleman to unravel the affairs of the Company. Mr. Sturge's character was well known, and he had given the accounts a thorough investigation.

Mr. Coleman.—Yes, but he has not told us the result.

Mr. Rowley.—He had offered Mr. Coleman a golden bridge over which he might escape if he chose; he did not, however, avail himself of it, but repeated a number of vague charges with which it was difficult to deal. The report of the committee stated that the additional money raised had been applied to the benefit of the Company.

Mr. Coleman.—Yes, by the *Company!*

Mr. Rowley.—And that on a cautious estimate of the landed property, &c.,

it was sufficient to meet the additional outlay. Mr. Coleman's object was to make an attack upon the Chairman of the Company.

Mr. Coleman.—Did the land not always belong to the Company? Are not my statements true? You accuse me of making vague charges. My statements are as direct as they can be.

Mr. Rowley said he had no confidence in them. It was provided by one of the clauses that no bondholder's interest could be affected without his consent, so that anything done to affect the Chairman's interest would, without his own consent in writing, be mere waste paper. In another clause it was stated, "the arrangement as regards the shareholders shall take effect when the shareholders have assented thereto." Yet Mr. Coleman stated that his investment was to be confiscated. He (Mr. Rowley) had no motive——

Mr. Coleman.—Except, confessedly, a money one. No moral motive.

Mr. Rowley had no motive but to support the Company as a mercantile investment. The directors were absolved by the committee's report, and he (Mr. Rowley) felt obliged to them for exceeding their parliamentary powers, since they had done it in the interests of the company.

Mr. Barrett asked when Mr. Rowley first saw the report of the committee.

Mr. Rowley said it was handed to him the night before the meeting.

Mr. Barrett.—Is it true that it was only circulated when the meeting was half over.

Mr. Rowley.—It is totally untrue.

Mr. Coleman.—Mr. Barrett is in error; I did not say so. I said it was circulated after the chairman had taken his seat. Will Mr. Rowley deny that?

Mr. Rowley said they were distributed before the chairman began.

Mr. Coleman.—I pledge my honor that these reports were not circulated till after the chairman had taken his seat and spoken.

Mr. Rowley said the chairman read every word of the reports. After dwelling upon the integrity and sagacity of Mr. Sturge, and contending that he would not sanction a misappropriation of the funds, he adverted to the Bill before Parliament, and recommended it to the support of the shareholders. He maintained that the directors ought to be supported, and that the resolutions passed at the meeting at Hartlepool, should be re-echoed by the shareholders at large.

Mr. Powell contended that Mr. Coleman's statements were uncandid and unfounded in fact. He admitted that there were some irregularities, but not to the extent that had been stated. He urged that Mr. Coleman was actuated by personal hostility to Mr. Jackson, and was not so entitled to credit as Mr. Sturge and the committee of assistance. It was well known, he said, to many proprietors, that there was a certain amount of unparliamentary capital. There had been no attempt at concealment, and what had been done was for the interest of the shareholders.

The Chairman.—We have heard certainly a considerable amount of speaking, but I do not find that any of the gentlemen who favored us with their opinions have really gone into the facts of the case. There has been a great deal said against Mr. Coleman, and there have been some little quiet friendly hits at me, but I hope I have behaved myself in a gentlemanly way: I have not intended to put forward these things at all offensively. I should have been very glad to hear something more about the state of these accounts: it is said that I am in a fog about them, and I confess I am in a fog, and nothing that these gentlemen have said has in any way tended to throw any light upon it. After all, assumptions are made that Mr. Sturge's account is a correct one; assumptions are made that the directors' report is a correct one; but I want facts and not assumptions. When I find that there is this enormous deficiency of £835,000, I do not want Mr. Powell to get up and tell the meeting and the shareholders that he supposes that that is bringing into account now, something that has been concealed during a long series of years. I want the directors to come forward in a straightforward manner, and tell us plainly in a few words, why these accounts have been concealed from the shareholders, and what has become of the books in which an account of all this has been kept. That is a plain straightforward explanation to ask for.

Mr. Rowley.—Mr. Sturge has had access to that.

The Chairman.—But he does not give us the means of judging; on the contrary, he carefully conceals it from us, and I think the way in which this account is put forward at the meeting, both Mr. Sturge's and the directors' account is not at all satisfactory, the accounts were put forward at a time when it was impossible to compare them with the Bill, and I think the shareholders have not been dealt with in a way that they have a right to expect. No one in this room is able to give any explanation, and nobody in this room being able to do so, I take upon myself to say that nobody else can, except Mr. Sturge and the directors, and they do not do it.

Mr. Rowley.—You live within a few doors of Mr. Bell, he will do it whenever you call upon him.

The Chairman.—You are very good to say so; I will try what I can do with Mr. Bell, with your recommendation added to my own. I *have* asked him for information, and I cannot get it from him; I asked him before and since the meeting. Now that you say so positively, that I can get it from Mr. Bell, I will make it my business to see if I can.

Mr. Rowley.—Will he not give you an explanation of this Bill?

The Chairman. He will not.

Mr. Rowley.—Does his explanation correspond with yours?

The Chairman.—I say he will not give an explanation of the Bill. Mr. Jackson's agents sent me the Bill; and when questions were asked, we are told, "this is the Bill of Mr. Sturge and the committee, you must ask Mr. Bell." Mr. Bell is not here, and Mr. Sturge is not here.

Mr. Rowley.—You know where to find Mr. Bell, he lives close to you.

The Chairman.—In order to show you that I am not quite so deficient in making inquiries at places where information can so readily be got, let me say that I did make it my business last Saturday to write a long letter to Mr. Bell, asking him for the particular information which Mr. Jackson said he would so readily give. Until this morning I got no answer from him, and now he refuses to give me any information at all; but on your recommendation I will try again. I will merely say, in conclusion, that if you are satisfied with the statement of accounts, or the non-statement of accounts, I am not satisfied until the accounts are furnished, and if any gentleman chooses to co-operate with me in any way, I shall be very glad of such co-operation. And, if not, I shall be very well content to do without it, and to seek redress in another way before a Committee of the House of Commons.

The meeting then terminated.

Messrs. Bell, Steward & Lloyd having written to offer to purchase Mr. Wilkinson's bonds, on behalf of Mr. Rowley—the following letters have passed:—

44, Lincoln's Inn Fields,
7th March, 1860.

Dear Sirs,—We are not less surprised at Mr. Rowley's bad memory of his twice-repeated words at the meeting, than at your still withholding the information; which, if it disclose an honest state of things, would silence us at once, and enable us to assure the shareholders of our satisfaction.

We leave you to judge how, in the face of the grave charges publicly made against the accounts, the refusal to satisfy us must be viewed by the public,

when coupled with the fact of the grave discrepancies in the published accounts, the surprising inuendos in the clauses of the Bill, and your and Mr. Sturge's studious absence from the meeting.

You refuse also to satisfy us now as to the meaning of the clauses and the amount of capital; but instead, you want to buy off our opposition by purchasing our debentures to the extent of £4,500.

We beg to inform you that we are now acting as the representatives and in concert with holders to the amount of £180,000, and to ask you if the purchase will extend to them also, and to others who are daily added to the list.

We draw your attention also to the fact, that the information we seek as to the accounts, extends to the sum of upwards of £1,000,000, being the increase asked for upon the amount published in February, 1859, at which time the committee was appointed.

This information is withheld from the shareholders and the bondholders; and if it be right to withhold it, it would be well to know the reason that can be given. How much better it would be to come forward at once with the accounts, and end all this doubt, and all these grave charges!

We remain, dear Sirs, yours faithfully,

YARBOROUGH & WILKINSON.

Messrs. Bell, Steward & Lloyd.

49, Lincoln's Inn Fields,
7th March, 1860.

West Hartlepool Harbour and Railway Company.

Dear Sirs,—We have received your letter of this day's date.

We repeat for the last time that the whole affairs of the Company have been investigated by a proper tribunal duly constituted, and they have pronounced a righteous verdict, the result of a year's labour.—The Company would not be called upon to go over the ground again with you even if they were satisfied of your fairness, or that you are not employed by parties having rival interests to the Company.

Your's faithfully,

BELL, STEWARD & LLOYD.

Messrs. Yarborough & Wilkinson.

44, Lincoln's Inn Fields,
8th March, 1860.

Dear Sirs,—We are sorry that our questions still elicit no direct reply, but only another statement that the affairs have been investigated, and a righteous verdict returned. We know they have been investigated, and what we ask is for a statement of the evidence on which the righteous verdict was returned. This is hardly an unreasonable request, when all we want is to know how our money has been dealt with.

The "proper tribunal" you speak of absented itself at the meeting, so that no inconvenient questions might be asked, and thus played into the hands of the person who is charged, whether rightly or wrongly, as the culprit.

Pray do not longer conceal the accounts from the shareholders and others interested; but in the interests of Mr. Jackson, prove him to have acted honestly.

Suppose, as you say, that we are specially employed by persons having rival interests to our Company, why do you by concealment give them and us such grounds of suspicion? If all is honest, disarm these rival parties whom you conjure up to lead us away from the sole issue in the case.

You do not inform us if Mr. Rowley is prepared to take up the interests of the other bondholders with whom we are acting.

Yours faithfully,

YARBOROUGH & WILKINSON.

Messrs. Bell, Steward & Lloyd.

POSTSCRIPT.

(*First Edition.*)

At the moment of going to press, I received the following note—which is instructive. Had Admiral Cator, to whom it refers, found a willing informant, he would probably have gone further, and have asked for some other particulars of my private arrangements.

14, *Great Winchester Street,*
6th March, 1860.

Dear Sir,

Perhaps in your controversy with the West Hartlepool Dock and Railway Company it may be useful for you to be informed that last year, previous to the time of the annual general meeting, a question was one day put to me in Gresham House, by Admiral Cator, and afterwards reiterated by his nephew, George Albemarle Cator, Esq., the Manager of the National Flax Company, but with what object I leave you to guess—a question of the amount of salary you allowed to my son, Samuel.

My reply was that I never had made any enquiries of my son on this particular point, because I had left him always to manage his own money affairs himself.

Evidently there was an invidious object in this very officious enquiry, and I considered at the time, that a question of this nature made to me was quite unworthy the high status of an admiral in the British Navy.

I only know and beg to assure you that any arrangements between you and my son, during the several years he has been in your counting house, have been perfectly satisfactory to my son and myself, and I take this opportunity of respectfully thanking you for the many proofs he has received of your kind and fatherly attention.

Always, dear Sir, yours truly,

JAMES HALDON.

To Benj. Coleman, Esq.

[The above is printed with the consent of the Writer.]

POSTSCRIPT.

(Second Edition.)

I HAVE now redeemed my pledge to you by petitioning against the Bill which sought to cover up the accounts of the Company, and compelling Mr. Jackson to withdraw it. Since the issue of the first edition of this pamphlet, the Board of Trade made their report to the House of Commons on the West Hartlepool Harbour and Railway Bill, in which the Bill is thoroughly dissected, and its remarkable clauses laid bare. For your information I now append a copy of this report, having placed in *italics* some of the strongest points, to which I invite your attention, and you will see how completely it corroborates the views expressed by Mr. Wilkinson, at the London Tavern Meeting, and how utterly unworthy such a Bill was of your support and how entirely prejudicial to your interests it would have been had it been permitted to pass. Fortunately, I and others had lodged our petition against the Bill, and had taken the necessary steps to compel the attendance of Mr. Jackson, Mr. Alfred Bell, and Mr. Sturge, who alone know the real state of the Company's affairs, and who on oath before a Committee of the House of Commons would have been obliged to disclose the real dealings with the Company's funds, and to have supplied the studied omissions of the Report of the Committee of Assistance. Mr. Jackson at the last moment found it not only prudent but necessary to withdraw the Bill. It is thus now plainly and openly admitted that the attempt to legalise and convert into bonds, having equal priority with such of yours as may be within the legal limits, the enormous sums which Mr. Jackson has spent in promoting his private speculations was an unjust and illegal proceeding, and one which would not bear the light.

For my own part, I regret exceedingly that Mr. Alfred Bell should have recommended or allowed his clients to withdraw the Bill, as the opportunity for the moment has been thereby lost of exposing more publicly, and to demonstration, transactions which I verily believe have no parallel in the annals of reckless adventure—in this country, at all events.

That the Company's accounts, as furnished by the directors and attested by Messrs. Fossick and Baynes, for years past, are entirely fallacious, and studiously conceal the real state of the funds and assets of the Company, there is no longer the smallest doubt.

I refer you to a pamphlet on the present financial position of the Company,* with the production of which I have had nothing to do, being wholly unacquainted with its able author, and to the report of Messrs. Gardner and Lovelock, public accountants employed by Messrs. Yarborough and Wilkinson, which I have here printed for your information, and I ask you whether, with such statements unrefuted—*deduced as they are entirely from the directors' own published reports and documents*—it is possible to come to any other conclusion than that the worst charges I have ever made against the administration of the West Hartlepool Company's affairs are literally true, and that the attempt on the part of Mr. Jackson, with the assistance of Mr. Thomas Sturge and Mr. Alfred Bell, to smuggle a Bill through Parliament, intended to whitewash the wrong-doer, is an act of culpability and injustice.

Mr. Sturge's Report tells you, that "on a very cautious estimate of the value of the *landed* property, the *securities* on the collieries, and the steam vessels, the Committee are of opinion that their present value exceeds the £500,000," by which the capital is over-

---

* *The present Financial Position of the West Hartlepool Company Considered.*—Baily Brothers, Cornhill.

topped, but there is now good reason to know that the excess is over £1,000,000.

Now the "*Landed Property*" ought not in common fairness to have been paraded here as a security for the amount of Mr. Jackson's deficiencies, because the land belonged *bona fide* to the Company, and whenever acquired, has already been charged in the accounts. If, as I think, it is prospectively the most valuable item for the security of the holders of *legitimate* debentures, you ought not to have been recommended by Mr. Sturge, to lessen your security by admitting holders of *illegal* debentures to the extent of a million sterling to rank with you, receiving as security, only for such concession, Mr. Jackson's collieries and steam vessels, which the Company for want of powers cannot hold and work, and which, if they could, would be as Mr. Jackson has already found them—ruinous to all concerned, and only useful to make a vamped-up show of traffic which has no real foundation of legitimate trading.

I told you on a former occasion, and I repeat it for the benefit of those who are not already acquainted with the fact, that the West Hartlepool Harbour and Railway Company is the only Company of any importance in the United Kingdom whose shares and debentures are not marketable in London, and have no place in the Stock Exchange price list; and this, be it remembered, has not been caused by anything I have said, but had existed long before I ventured to raise my voice upon the subject, and still exists.

You will recollect that at the general meeting of 1859, I stated, in proof of the little confidence, which those best acquainted with the condition of the Company's affairs had, in the soundness of its position and its prospects, that several of the former directors seceded without any remark being made, and that one of them, Mr. Richard Fenwick, had sold his stock at about 30 per cent. discount.

Mr. Fenwick, who was present, thought himself justified in flatly contradicting me, but nevertheless my statement was substantially correct. He had not *sold* his shares at 30 per cent. discount it is true; but when Mr. Jackson heard of his determination to sell them, he offered to *exchange* them for debentures, which Mr. Fenwick accepted, and a price was fixed of somewhere between 20 and 30 per cent. discount. Mr. Fenwick has since parted with the greatest portion of these debentures, and recently he has been pleased to express himself to the effect, that I am entitled to the gratitude of the shareholders for having dragged out the fact, now first admitted, that the Company was ruinously involved in colliery and steam boat speculations, which Mr. Jackson had assured him over and over again it had nothing to with.

Admitting, as Mr. Jackson now asserts, that the Company are really the owners of collieries and steam boats, "and have been so since 1853"—and admitting, as Mr. Sturge's report does, that there is a present deficit of £500,000 at least, but if the accounts were looked into probably of more than double that amount, on these illegal and unauthorized speculations, it is clear that to secure a nett revenue of little more than £100,000, Mr. Jackson has spent £70,000 per annum for the last seven years which he has entirely concealed from you in his accounts. If he had brought this forward it would have left him without the means of paying any dividend on his stock, and with only half the amount required to pay interest on his preference shares and debenture debt, against which however he would be entitled to set off the value, whatever that may be, of the collieries and steam boats, and which I am credibly informed, is not one half of the *admitted* deficiency.

Surely this is a state of things to which you cannot remain indifferent.

That an enormous sum of money beyond the Company's parliamentary powers has been raised and spent, and is now sought to be concealed from you, appears to be indubitable. THE QUESTION IS, HOW HAS IT BEEN RAISED? If by bonds, then clearly the holders of such securities have no claim whatever on the property of the Company, and they will therefore do well to call on Messrs. Sturge, Jackson, and Bell, to clear up this point at once; but everything like an open exposition of the Company's accounts is studiously avoided. Mr. Jackson, be it remembered, never had an open shareholders' meeting until I forced him to admit reporters. Then, to save himself from the necessity of answering at once, the charges I had publicly made against the management of the Company, he adroitly drew around him a number of respectable men, whom he had privately canvassed, and making a show of candour, offered to submit the Company's accounts to a Committee, which, as I have previously said, was nominated by himself and was composed of men he believed would never act. Thereupon, and without waiting for the result of an enquiry, which would have been the more fitting time for praise, complimentary resolutions were passed and duly advertised, and the press was set to work to give a garbled and entirely false version of the Company's position.

At that moment Mr. Sturge stepped in, in the manner I have described, with an evident determination to unravel the web, and I believe he did in a great measure unravel it; but when the shareholders were expecting a candid *exposé*, after twelve months investigation, he, by some mysterious influence, turned aside from the discharge of his duty, and gave a report which confessed nothing but that there is a grand deficit of at least half a million, even as he puts it, but in reality this deficit, as I have said, is over £1,000,000; and he recommended a Bill to empower the Company to raise more capital, without condescending to give "the reason why." Upon this Mr. Jackson weaves with unusual ingenuity and disengenuousness, Mr. Sturge's Report, with his own Annual Report to the Shareholders, and brings out a flourishing result for "the admirers of judicious enterprise." Again resolutions were passed of a *specially* complimentary character, and of course advertised, to keep up the delusion.

A day of reckoning, however, as some day come it must, seemed to be at hand. The Bill was, unfortunately for them, to come before a Committee of the House of Commons, and the opportunity would thus at last be given, to go into the Company's accounts, and obtain the long demanded explanations, of how the money had been spent, and whether or not it had been raised by the issue of illegal bonds. But again we were doomed to some disappointment, for at the moment the committee were ready to hear the case, and counsel and witnesses were all ready to go into the allegations of my petition, Mr. Jackson and his adviser, Mr. Bell, turned faint-hearted, and deeming "discretion to be the better part of valour," withdrew the Bill, and confessed thereby that *they dare not* submit the real state of the Company's accounts to the scrutiny of an impartial tribunal. This, however, is a great victory for you, which I shall know how to use for your benefit. It was as you will find, "the beginning of the end."

Truly it was a serious day for Mr. Jackson, when in the face of my petition, he found it necessary to withdraw the bill, and thus throw up his cards, and tacitly admit the charges made against him. It does not say much for railway management, that he was not compelled at the same moment to retire from all connexion with the Company, but this, too, must follow at no distant day. Still it was necessary for him to put some front upon the direful circumstances in which he is placed, and it is instructive for you to read his words announcing the shipwreck to the public. The day following the withdrawal of the bill, the following paragraph appeared in the *Railway Times* and other papers, and as no pen but Mr. Jackson's is equal to such writing, it is well for him to have the credit of its authorship:—

"WEST HARTLEPOOL.

"The bill suggested by the committee of assistance, and approved by the shareholders at their late meeting, *having been considered by the authorities of Parliament,* it has been intimated to the promoters that the bill in its present shape could not be properly proceeded with, *in consequence of the Company possessing so large an amount of landed property and assets,* greatly exceeding in value *the additional amount expended for promoting the interests and rapid development of the undertaking.* As, therefore, further capital is not as yet required for any increased permanent works, and would be no longer requisite when the landed property *and assets of the Company* are realised, the promoters have been advised that Parliamentary powers are not necessary for additional capital of only a temporary character, and hence the bill is not to be proceeded with in the present session."

So that he wishes you to think that it was by no means a want of money which made him go to Parliament, but only that the grand discovery was made when he got there, that he had too much of assets, and that this plethora must be reduced before next year.

I am able, however, to give you some information as to what was the result of the Bill "having been considered by Parliament." Unfortunately for us, it was not that we have too large assets, but that in the face of enormous and pressing liabilities of over £,1000,000, there is £490,000 share capital unsubscribed, and which cannot be got out on the market, and Lord Redesdale, I believe, amongst other private questions, asked Mr. Jackson how he could think of coming for increased capital powers whilst such a sum had been for years unexhausted. There were other questions asked by Lord Redesdale, and Mr. Jackson was told that if he did not give an immediate and satisfactory answer, he must at once withdraw the Bill—*and Mr. Jackson withdrew it accordingly.*

The striking Report of the Board of Trade hits all these blots and many more. Such a document has, I venture to say, hardly ever been issued before from that admirable department, *and it was on the table of the committee.* It is only needful to say that the Bill could not remain there long by the side of such a report.

To the debenture holders, I will only say, that it being now publicly demonstrated by the Report of the Board of Trade that there is an acknowledged over-issue of bonds to the extent of £150,000, and as I believe to a much greater amount, it behoves you not to allow your bonds to be renewed until the Company is brought again within the limits of its borrowing powers, or you will incur the risk of holding worthless pieces of paper. *It is however a most alarming circumstance for the poor bondholders to know that there are already in their hands, at the very least,* £150,000 *of worthless debentures, and probably, even worthless debentures to three times that amount.*

To the shareholders, I say, that at once you should insist on the appointment of an independent committee of investigation, who shall deal with a strong hand with the actual state of the Company, and that such committee shall come before you with a full statement of your affairs, and an honest Bill to place them on a better footing. No concealment of the real state of things can either be allowed, or be of avail now. Too much has been exposed, and too many admissions have been extorted, to make concealment any longer desirable or practicable.

There is in the meantime another course open to me, which will be taken to get at some of the West Hartlepool Harbour and Railway Company's accounts, and to do you partial justice. But you will doubtless weigh well the gravity of the Company's and your own position. You will not omit to look to the pamphlet I have before named. You will be sure to ask yourselves how is it that I am permitted to make with impunity these broad and damning charges? How is it that I am not *compelled* by law proceedings to prove them? How is it that all who are interested do not insist on having them swept away? I will tell you. There is no answer which can be given. The statements are unmistakeably true, and those who know the real state of the Company, "have marched through Coventry" with Mr. Jackson too long to make it possible for them to take up the position in these affairs, which, as men of character, they ought only to occupy. To Mr. Bell's known influence over Mr. Sturge is to be found the solution, no doubt, of that gentleman's swerving from the fulfilment of a duty he had voluntarily undertaken; and thus it has been Mr. Jackson's fortune so far to elude detection when it appeared imminent and certain. But every plot has its catastrophe, and you will find that Mr. Jackson's tortuous career will afford no exception to the general rule.

BENJ. COLEMAN.

March 30th, 1860.

RAILWAY AND CANAL BILLS.

FURTHER REPORT from the Board of Trade, in compliance with an Order of the Honorable The House of Commons, dated 26th January, 1860.

"That the Board of Trade do present to this House a Report upon the Railway and Canal Bills of this Session, in compliance with the Recommendation contained in the Fifth Report of the Select Committee on Railway and Canal Bills of the Session of 1853."

West Hartlepool Harbour and Railway Bill.

THE objects of this Bill appear to be to enable the West Hartlepool Harbour and Railway Company, by arrangement with their creditors and shareholders, to effect a division of their capital and debt into railway capital and debenture debt and Harbour and Docks capital and debenture debt; to increase the amount of the authorised capital and loan from £2,686,080 to £3,400,000, of which £2,000,000 is to be the amount of the railway capital and loan; *to confirm mortgages and bonds already issued by the Company in anticipation* of such increased loan powers; and to make provision with respect to lien for freight on goods landed at the Company's works.

In the preamble of this Bill, page 10, the present authorised aggregate capital of the Company is stated at £2,014,560, which corresponds with the definition of their capital in the C ompany's Act of 1857, and their loan is stated at £671,520.

With respect to the latter amount it is to be observed that, previously to the passing of the Act of 1857, the loan power ofthe Company w as limited to £521,520; that by the Act of 1857 additional capital to the amount of £450,000 was authorised to be raised by means of shares; but no further borrowing power was expressly given by that Act. It would seem, therefore, that the Company claim to have been authorised in 1857 to raise an additional sum of £150,000 by borrowing, in respect of the additional share capital of £450,000, by reason of there being in their Act of 1852 (c. 142, s. 85), a provision empowering them to borrow to the amount of one-third of their capital in stock and shares for the time being. *It appears questionable*, however, whether that provision, which requires all moneys borrowed under it to be applied solely to the purposes of the Act of 1852, could have been intended to give a general power to borrow to the amount of one-third of all additional share capital that might be authorised by any subsequent Act relating to the Company; and in the preamble of the Act of 1857, £450,000 and not £600,000 *is mentioned as the further capital* which it was expedient that the Company should be authorized to raise.

In addition to the sum of £600,000 which the Company claim to have been authorized to raise by their Act of 1857, they seek by the present Bill to be empowered to create share and loan capital to the further amount of £713,920, to make up £3,400,000, which is stated in page 9 to be "the aggregate amount which the Company have laid out, or are in the course of expending, or must necessarily expend upon the undertaking."

With reference to the largely extended money powers sought by this Bill, it may be observed that the railways of the Company authorised previously to the Act of 1857 (45 miles in length) had been completed before 31st December, 1856. No extension of the Company's railways or harbour was authorised by the Act of 1857, or subsequently; and by the preamble of that Act, it appears that the further capital of £450,000 was then considered sufficient "to meet and provide for the cost of additional "docks, shipping staiths, wharfs and warehouses, piers, harbour and sea-"works, urgently required to be undertaken, and now in progress, for the "accommodation of commerce, and the refuge, safety, and convenience of "shipping and mariners, and also for additional sidings, engines, carriages, "waggons, and other railway working stock for providing and carrying on "a greatly increasing traffic."

No extension of the Company's railways or harbour is proposed to be authorised by this Bill; and it may be a matter for inquiry whether the Company's powers for executing works have not expired by lapse of time. It would therefore seem to *require investigation what has been the nature of the outlay*, which will exceed the £450,000 considered as sufficient in 1857, not only by the additional sum of £150,000, which the Company appear to have borrowed under a supposed authority from the Act of 1857, but also by further sums amounting to £713,920, for which liabilities have been or are being incurred by the Company, in anticipation of the powers sought for in this Bill.

With respect to the statement of capital in page 8 of this Bill, it may be observed that it does not appear how much of the capitals of £526,400 and £450,000, authorised by the Acts of 1852 and 1857, has been paid up; and it might be desirable on the present occasion that the amount remaining unpaid should be ascertained; more especially, as by Section 14, it is proposed to extinguish to some extent the powers of the Company under their existing Acts of raising money by, and creating shares and stock; and *from Section* 28, it would seem that mortgages and bonds have been issued for raising capital which might have been raised by preferential and ordinary consolidated shares and stocks not fully paid up.

It is stated in the preamble, page 9, that "the Company are the owners "of a considerable extent of land in and near to West Hartlepool, of which "land it is essential that they should have the command as ballast ground:" and it appears to be intended to dispose of such land as building ground, and in the meanwhile to constitute it, and also "*other property* of the Company connected with the Harbour and Docks" (page 11), as security for money raised and to be raised in respect of the Harbour and Docks.

Inasmuch as under the proposed provisions of this Bill, the Harbour and Docks debenture debt may form a large proportion of the intended Harbour and Docks capital and loan of £1,400,000, it appears to be of importance that the *particulars, cost price, and estimated future value of the "ballast ground," and "other property* of the Company connected with the Harbour and Docks," *should be fully inquired into.*

By Sections 30 and 31 of the Bill the proceeds of sale of the ballast ground and property of the Company connected with the Harbour and Docks are made applicable towards satisfaction of the Harbour and Docks debenture debt; and Section 32 requires that separate accounts shall be kept of the moneys raised by such sale. It may deserve consideration whether the "ballast ground and *other property* connected with the Harbour and Docks" should not be so described in the Bill *as to be capable of being identified;* for in the absence of any further description than the Bill now contains, neither the creditors nor the shareholders would have the means of ascertaining whether the proceeds of sale of the ballast ground and other property will have been brought into account, and applied in the manner required by Sections 30–32.

And it would seem to be essential to the proper carrying into effect the division of the undertaking of the Company into a Railway Undertaking, and a Harbour and Docks Undertaking, with separate classes of creditors holding securities, and of preferential and ordinary shareholders, as proposed in this Bill, that provision should be made for *a clear division and allotment* of the property of the Company between the two undertakings.

The Bill, however, does not appear to contain any provision for that purpose.

Sections 18 and 22.—The effect of these clauses appears to be to leave the proportion which the harbour and docks capital and debenture debt may bear to each other so far undefined, as virtually to authorise the Company to *borrow nearly the whole of the* £1,400,000, which is proposed to be the aggregate amount of such capital and debenture debt.

For the present authorised share capital of the Company is £2,014,560, of which a part appears by Section 28 not to have been paid up in full. There is no provision in the Bill rendering necessary the creation of any additional *share capital* for raising the further funds to be authorised by the Bill; and the railway capital, under Sections 17 and 21, is to include at least £1,500,000. Consequently the harbour and docks capital need not in any case exceed £514,560, which would be the surplus of the present authorised share capital, after allotting £1,500,000 to the railway capital; *and the whole of the difference* between £1,400,000 and £514,560 (*i. e.*, £885,440) might *be borrowed as Harbour and Docks debenture debt* under Sections 18 and 22.

It may further be observed, that there does not appear to be anything in the Bill to prevent an "arrangement" between *the Company and the shareholders,* by which the whole of the £2,000,000 of intended railway capital shall consist of share capital, so as to leave only £14,560 of the present authorised share capital to constitute the Harbour and Docks capital; and in that case the proposed provisions of Sections 18 and 22 would enable the Company to have, as Harbour and Docks debenture debt, *the whole of the difference* between £1,400,000 and 14,560, *i. e.*, £1,385,440.

The last-mentioned sum is the amount which the Company would be authorised by the Bill to have on loan on the security either of the Harbour and Docks alone, or partly of the Harbour and Docks and partly of the railway; and it exceeds considerably the limit of loan capital fixed by the West Hartlepool Harbour and Railway Act, 1852, *viz.*, one-third of the Company's share capital. It seems questionable whether the proposed increase of the Company's borrowing powers, without any increase of share capital, *will be justified by the grounds* which appear to be *alleged* in that behalf in the preamble, pages 10 and 11, *viz.*, that the Harbour and Docks of the Company are of the nature of a public undertaking, which, if intrusted by Parliament to commissioners or trustees, would have been executed by means of borrowed money; and that the Company have ballast ground *and other property* which they consider to form a valuable security for money laid out in respect of the Harbour and Docks.

Sections 27, 34, 35. It appears to be essential to the carrying into effect of the objects of these clauses that the Bill should contain, or make provision for, some further definition of the "undertaking *and property* in respect of the railway," and "the undertaking *and property* in respect of the Harbour and Docks."

Section 28 appears to have for its object the *legalising all mortgages and bonds which the Company may have issued* before the passing of the Bill in *excess of their present powers.* Such excess may include not only the sum of £713,920, which is the difference between £3,400,000, and the present authorised capital and loan of £2,686,080 stated in the preamble, page 8, but also the sum of £150,000, if erroneously assumed to have been raiseable by loan, under the Act of 1857, and *any sums which may have been raised by loan instead of by calls, in respect of the amount not paid up on the preferential and ordinary consolidated shares and stock* of the Company.

The extent and the grounds of the excessive issues of mortgages and bonds thus sought to be legalised, and the *application which has been made of the monies thereby raised*, will doubtless undergo full investigation by the Committee on this Bill.

My Lords have thought it right to call attention to the above points. At the same time they would observe that the great and rapid increase of trade at Hartlepool in recent years, which is adverted to in the Bill, may not unreasonably be supposed to have led to an amount of expenditure not at first anticipated, and which, so far as it is connected with railway harbour and dock purposes, may perhaps be explained by that circumstance.

Section 33.—It appears to be a question whether the liabilities referred to in this clause *may exceed, or must be within* the proposed aggregate capital and loan of £3,400,000, and what is *intended to be the effect*, in point of charge or security, of their being "*attributed*" by the Company to or in respect of their railway and their harbour and docks respectively.

If it be intended by this clause to *give to such liabilities any increased validity*, it might be proper to confine the recognition of them in the Bill to liabilities incurred *for purposes authorised by the Company's Acts.*

Section 67.—The words "for the delivery," in the sixth line of this clause appear to be erroneous. Perhaps the words "of the warehousing or depositing" were intended to be used.

In Section 71 it might be proper to qualify the words "for all purposes," by the addition of the words "of this Act," as in Section 68.

Section 72 appears to require amendment, by inserting after the words "tolls, dues, and charges on shipping" the words "or on goods carried in ships;" by changing "for," in the sixth line of the clause, into "from;" and by omitting "thereof" in the same line.

JAMES BOOTH.

Board of Trade—March 1860.

To Messrs. Yarborough and Wilkinson,
44, Lincoln's-inn Fields.

44, Basinghall Street, E. C.,
15th March, 1860.

West Hartlepool Harbour and Railway Company.

Gentlemen,—In compliance with your instructions we have carefully examinined the published Reports and Accounts of this Company, and beg

to call your attention to the following grave circumstances in connection therewith, *viz.*—

1*st*.—That the Committee of Assistance state the parliamentary powers of the Company to have been exceeded by "about" £500,000.

The share capital and liabilities would therefore stand thus—

Amount of parliamentary power - -				£2,686,080	0 0
Excess, as per Committee's Report, about				500,000	0 0
Together - - -				£3,186,080	0 0
While according to the Directors' Report for 1859, the amount raised appears to be—					
On shares - -	1,575,154	10	11		
Mortgage debenture account - -	671,520	0	0		
				2,246,674	10 11
Shewing liabilities in addition to the authorised debenture loans of about -				£939,405	9 1

2*nd*.—That there is no information as to the periods at which this enormous sum has been raised; the rate of interest paid for the same; or, what securities are held by the creditors representing that amount.

3*rd*.—That the amount thus due, about - -	£939,405	0	0
And the amount due on mortgage debenture account - - - - - - -	671,520	0	0
Together - - -	£1,610,925	0	0
Exceed the total amount raised on shares of every description, *viz.* - - -	£1,575,154	10	11

4*th*.—That the Company now seek parliamentary powers to raise additional share capital, although their present powers for that purpose amount to - - - - - - -	£2,014,560	0	0
Of which, on 31st December, 1859, they had only received - - - - -	1,575,154	10	11
Leaving unexhausted - - -	£439,405	9	1

5*th*.—That the interest, (if any) received by the Company on the following items which appear in the 1859 Report, *viz.*:—

"Balance owing to the Company on securities - - - - - - -	£403,016	18	6
"Cleveland Railway Account - -	46,382	5	11
"North-Eastern Railway Company's 4 per cent. preference stock - -	40,640	0	0
Together - - -	£490,039	4	5"

Is nowhere stated in the published accounts.

6th.—That the items in the "Summary of Balance Sheet, 31st December 1859," are so obscurely stated as to conceal from the shareholders the information they should contain as to the position of the Company.

7th.—That previously to the issuing of the Report for December, 1859, no trace of the Company having exceeded its powers for capital could be discovered from any of the reports or accounts published by the Company.

8th.—That the non-discovery of these important matters by the Auditors who have acted for the last few years, shews those gentlemen to have been remiss in their duties, and that their signatures cannot be received as indicative of the correctness of any of the accounts.

We have the honour to be, Gentlemen,

Your obedient servants,

GARDNER & LOVELOCK,

Public Accountants.

PRINTED BY THOMAS SCOTT, WARWICK COURT, HOLBORN.

CPSIA information can be obtained
at www.ICGtesting.com
Printed in the USA
BVHW042323110819
555626BV00017B/4705/P

9 781318 096046